uncovered editions

BLOODY SUNDAY, 1972

LORD WIDGERY'S REPORT OF

EVENTS IN LONDONDERRY,

NORTHERN IRELAND,

ON 30 JANUARY 1972

∞⊙✕⊙∞

London: The Stationery Office

© The Stationery Office 2001

Applications for reproduction should be made in writing to
The Stationery Office Limited, St Crispins, Duke Street,
Norwich NR3 1PD.

ISBN 0 11 702405 8
First published as *Report of the Tribunal appointed to inquire into
the events on Sunday, 30th January 1972, which led to loss of life in
connection with the procession in Londonderry on that day by
The Rt. Hon. Lord Widgery, OBE, TD* (HMSO, 1972).
© Crown copyright

A CIP catalogue record for this book is available from the
British Library.

Cover photograph © Hulton Getty.

Typeset by J&L Composition Ltd, Filey, North Yorkshire.

Printed in the United Kingdom for The Stationery Office by
Biddles Ltd, Guildford, Surrey.
TJ3384   C30   2/01

COMHAIRLE CHONTAE ÁTHA CLIATH THEAS
SOUTH DUBLIN COUNTY LIBRARIES

LUCAN LIBRARY
TO RENEW ANY ITEM TEL: 621 6422

Items should be returned on or before the last date below. Fines, as displayed in the Library, will be charged on overdue items.

19. JUL. 01.		

Other titles in the *uncovered editions* series

The Amritsar Massacre: General Dyer in the Punjab, 1919
The Boer War: Ladysmith and Mafeking, 1900
British Battles of World War I, 1914–15
The British Invasion of Tibet: Colonel Younghusband, 1904
Defeat at Gallipoli: the Dardanelles Commission Part II,
    1915–16
D Day to VE Day: General Eisenhower's Report, 1944–45
Florence Nightingale and the Crimea, 1854-55
The Irish Uprising, 1914–21
John Profumo and Christine Keeler, 1963
The Judgement of Nuremberg, 1946
Lord Kitchener and Winston Churchill: The Dardanelles
    Commission Part I, 1914–15
The Loss of the Titanic, 1912
R.101: the Airship Disaster, 1930
Rillington Place
The Russian Revolution, 1917
The Siege of Kars, 1855
The Siege of the Peking Embassy, 1900
The Strange Story of Adolf Beck
Tragedy at Bethnal Green
Travels in Mongolia, 1902
UFOs in the House of Lords, 1979
War 1914: Punishing the Serbs
War 1939: Dealing with Adolf Hitler
Wilfrid Blunt's Egyptian Garden: Fox-hunting in Cairo

Forthcoming titles

Escape from Germany, 1939–45
Guezo, King of Dahomey, 1850–52
Letters of Henry VIII, 1526–29
War in the Falklands, 1982

Uncovered Editions are historic official papers which have not previously been available in a popular form. The series has been created directly from the archive of The Stationery Office in London. This book contains the text of Lord Widgery's original report.

Series editor: Tim Coates

Tim Coates studied at University College, Oxford and at the University of Stirling. After working in the theatre for a number of years, he took up bookselling and became managing director, firstly of Sherratt and Hughes bookshops, and then of Waterstone's. He is known for his support for foreign literature, particularly from the Czech Republic. The idea for 'Uncovered Editions' came while searching through the bookshelves of his late father-in-law, Air Commodore Patrick Cave OBE. He is married to Bridget Cave, has two sons, and lives in London.

Tim Coates welcomes views and ideas on the Uncovered ditions series. He can be e-mailed at timcoatesbooks@yahoo.com.

On Sunday 30 January, a protest march organised by the Northern Ireland Civil Rights Association took place in Londonderry, Northern Ireland, in the area of the Bogside and Creggan Estate. During the afternoon of that march, 13 civilians were killed by British soldiers, and another 13 were injured. As a result, a tribunal was appointed to inquire into the events which led up to this tragic loss of life. Heading the inquiry was Lord Widgery. The text which follows is his report.

Ireland, 1972

INTRODUCTION

APPOINTMENT OF TRIBUNAL

On Sunday 30 January 1972 British soldiers opened fire in the streets of Londonderry. Thirteen civilians lost their lives and a like number were injured; their names are listed overleaf:

DEAD

Patrick Joseph Doherty
Gerald Donaghy
John Francis Duddy
Hugh Pius Gilmore
Michael Kelly
Michael McDaid
Kevin McElhinney

Bernard McGuigan
Gerald McKinney
William Anthony
  McKinney
William Noel Nash
James Joseph Wray
John Pius Young

INJURED

Michael Bradley
Michael Bridge
Patrick Campbell
Margaret Deery
Damien Donaghy
Joseph Friel
John Johnson

Joseph Mahon
Patrick McDaid
Daniel McGowan
Alexander Nash
Patrick O'Donnell
Michael Quinn

On the following day I accepted an invitation from Her Majesty's Government to conduct a Tribunal of Inquiry into these events. Both Houses of Parliament adopted a Resolution in the following terms on 1 February:

> That it is expedient that a Tribunal be established
> for inquiring into a definite matter of urgent public

importance, namely the events on Sunday
30 January which led to loss of life in connection
with the procession in Londonderry on that day.

In order to ensure that the powers vested in the
Tribunal would extend to transferred matters under
the Government of Ireland Act, 1920, as well as to
matters reserved to Westminster, a Resolution in
identical terms was adopted in both Houses of the
Northern Ireland Parliament. The Home Secretary,
The Right Honourable Reginald Maudling, signed
a Warrant of Appointment on 2 February. The
Warrant declared that the Tribunals of Inquiry
(Evidence) Act, 1921 should apply to the Tribunal
and that the Tribunal was constituted as a Tribunal
within the meaning of that Act. A Warrant of
Appointment in identical terms was signed by the
Governor of Northern Ireland, Lord Grey, on 4
February. The Secretary to the Tribunal was
appointed on 6 February and left at once for
Northern Ireland. Meanwhile the Treasury
Solicitor's Department had already started taking
statements from witnesses in London.

TERMS OF REFERENCE

The terms of reference of the Inquiry were as stated
in the Parliamentary Resolutions and the Warrants

of Appointment. At a preliminary hearing on 14 February I explained that my interpretation of those terms was that the Inquiry was essentially a fact-finding exercise, by which I meant that its purpose was to reconstruct, with as much detail as was necessary, the events which led up to the shooting of a number of people in the streets of Londonderry on the afternoon of Sunday 30 January. The Tribunal was not concerned with making moral judgments; its task was to try and form an objective view of the events and the sequence in which they occurred, so that those who were concerned to form judgments would have a firm basis on which to reach their conclusions. The Tribunal would, therefore, listen to witnesses who were present on the occasion and who could assist in reconstructing the events from the evidence of what they saw with their own eyes or heard with their own ears. I wished to hear evidence from people who supported each of the versions of the events of 30 January which had been given currency.

I emphasised the narrowness of the confines of the Inquiry, the value of which would largely depend on its being conducted and concluded expeditiously. If considerations not directly relevant to the matters under review were allowed to take up time, the production of the Tribunal's Report would be delayed. The limits of the Inquiry in space were the streets of Londonderry in which the disturbances and the shooting took place; in time, the period beginning with the moment when the march first became involved in violence and ending with the deaths of the deceased and the conclusion of the affair.

At the first substantive hearing I explained that the emphasis on the importance of eye witnesses did not exclude evidence such as that of pathologists. Nor did it exclude consideration of the orders given to the Army before the march. The officers who conceived the orders and made the plans, including those for the employment of the 1st Battalion of the Parachute Regiment, would appear before me.

CHOICE OF LOCATION

My original intention was to hold the Inquiry in Londonderry, since if it were held anywhere else the people of Londonderry might be inhibited from giving evidence. For reasons of security and convenience I reluctantly concluded that other possibilities would have to be considered; and several were. In the end I decided on Coleraine, which had these advantages: it was only about 30 miles from Londonderry, to which it was linked by a good train service; and the County Hall, which the Londonderry County Council kindly put at my disposal, was admirably suited to the job. Nowhere else in the area, except in the City of Londonderry itself, was a suitable building available. The Council Chamber, in which the Tribunal sat, contained an adequate public gallery, so that there was proper accommodation for the public, who, with the Press, were admitted to the hearings.

SESSIONS OF THE TRIBUNAL

The first substantive hearing of the Tribunal was held on 21 February and I continued to sit in Coleraine until 14 March. During these 17 sessions 114 witnesses gave evidence and were cross-examined. The witnesses, who are listed at the end of the Report, fell into six main groups: priests; other people from Londonderry; press and television reporters, photographers, cameramen and sound recordists; soldiers, including the relevant officers; police officers; doctors, forensic experts and pathologists. After all the evidence had been taken, three further sessions were held in the Royal Courts of Justice in London on 16, 17 and 20 March, at which I heard the closing speeches of Counsel for the relatives of the deceased, for the Army and for the Tribunal.

REPRESENTATION OF RELATIVES' INTERESTS

Initially there was some doubt as to whether the residents of Londonderry would be prepared to come and give evidence at the Tribunal at all. This was a matter of some concern. As the Army was to be represented by leading Counsel it was highly desirable that other interests should be represented on the same level so that cross-examination of the Army witnesses should not devolve on Counsel for the Tribunal alone. In the event this need was met by my granting legal representation to the relatives of the deceased and to those injured in the shooting, whose interest in the matter embraced that of the citizens of Londonderry generally.

SOURCES OF EVIDENCE

A large quantity of material had to be examined. As has been mentioned above, the number of witnesses called was 114; but a much larger number of statements, roughly double that number, was taken, all of which were considered in arriving at a decision as to the witnesses to be called. This was in addition to the statements taken from the soldiers by the Royal Military Police on the night of 30 to 31 January. The Northern Ireland Civil Rights Association collected a large number of statements from people in Londonderry said to be willing to give evidence. These statements reached me at an advanced stage in the Inquiry. In so far as they contained new material, not traversing ground already familiar from evidence given before me, I have made use of them. Seven of the wounded appeared before the Tribunal and gave evidence. I did not think it necessary to take evidence from those of the wounded who were still in hospital. A particularly valuable feature of the evidence was the large number of photographs taken by professional photographers who had gone to Londonderry to cover the march.* Since it was obvious that by giving evidence soldiers and police officers might increase the dangers which they, and indeed their families, have to run, I agreed that they should appear before me under pseudonyms. This arrangement did not apply to the senior officers, who are well known in Northern Ireland. Except for the senior officers, the individual soldiers and police officers are referred to in my Report by the letter or number under which they gave evidence in the Tribunal.

* Photographs not included with this Report.

NARRATIVE OF EVENTS

LONDONDERRY: THE PHYSICAL BACKGROUND

The City of Londonderry; second in Ulster only to
Belfast in size and importance, lies on both banks of
the River Foyle. The events with which the

Londonderry, 1972

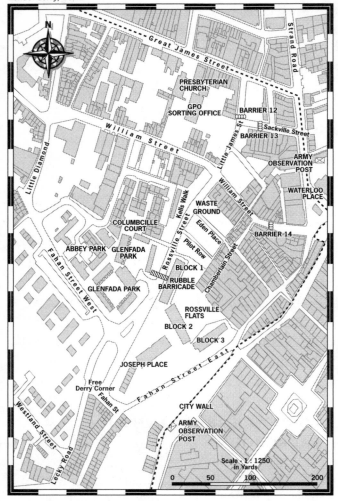

Tribunal was primarily concerned took place on the west bank, and indeed wholly within an area about a quarter of a mile square, bounded on the north by Great James Street, on the east by Strand Road, Waterloo Place and the City Wall, on the south by Free Derry Corner and Westland Street and on the west by Fahan Street West and the Little Diamond. (Free Derry Corner is the name popularly given to the junction of Lecky Road, Rossville Street and Fahan Street.) This area, which is shown on the map and is in the north-east corner of the Bogside district, is overlooked from the south-east side by the western section of the City's ancient Walls, which encircle the old heart of the town and which have major significance in Orange tradition because of the successful defence of Londonderry against James II; and from the west by the Creggan, a largely new district built on rising ground. Creggan and the old town look at one another across the Bogside. The Bogside and Creggan are predominantly Catholic districts, their population amounting to about 33,000 out of a total population in the City of Londonderry of about 55,000. The Bogside contains a number of old terraced houses and buildings, many of them derelict or nearly so; but also a large number of new blocks of flats and maisonettes. The small area with which the Tribunal was concerned lies on flat ground at a meeting point of old and new buildings. William Street is now largely derelict; and Chamberlain Street is an older street of terraced houses. Eden Place and Pilot Row do not contain any buildings at all; they are merely the sites of former streets which have been completely cleared of buildings. All the flats so frequently mentioned in evidence—the Rossville Flats, Glenfada Park, Kells Walk, Columbcille Court, Abbey Park and Joseph Place—are very modern buildings. The Rossville Flats consist of three blocks each of about 10 storeys high. The others are all low blocks. A notable feature of the area is that it contains a number of large open spaces which have been cleared of buildings, on both sides of William Street and of Rossville Street, as well as the courtyards and the open spaces arising from the layout of the new blocks of flats.

EVENTS IN LONDONDERRY DURING THE PREVIOUS SIX MONTHS

The Bogside and the Creggan, the Republican views of whose people are well known, were the scene of large-scale rioting in 1969 and have suffered sporadic rioting by hooligans ever since. In the early summer of 1971 a good deal of progress had been made towards restoring normal life. The Royal Ulster Constabulary was patrolling almost everywhere in the area on foot, the Army was little in evidence, the hooligan element had been isolated and the IRA was quiescent. At the beginning of July, however, gunmen appeared and an IRA campaign began. Widespread violence ensued with the inevitable military counter-action. Nevertheless at the end of August it was decided, after consultation with a group of prominent local citizens, to reduce the level of military activity in the hope that moderate opinion would prevail and the IRA gunmen be isolated from the community.

From the end of August to the end of October an uneasy equilibrium was maintained. In a conscious effort to avoid provocation the Army made itself less obvious. Though parts of the Bogside and Creggan were patrolled, no military initiative was taken except in response to aggression or for specific search or arrest operations. The improvement hoped for did not, however, take place. The residents of the Bogside and Creggan threw up or repaired over 50 barricades, including the one in Rossville Street which figured prominently in the proceedings of the Inquiry; frequent sniping and bombing attacks were made on the security forces; and the IRA tightened its grip on the district. Thus although at the end of October the policy was still one of passive containment, sniping and bombing had become increasingly common in virtually the whole of Londonderry west of the River Foyle. The Royal Ulster Constabulary had not operated in the Bogside and Creggan since June or July. Apart from one Company location at the Blighs Lane factory in the centre of the area, all military posts were located round the edges of the district. So the law was not effectively enforced in the area.

At the end of October, 8 Infantry Brigade, within whose area of command the City of Londonderry lay, was given instructions progressively to regain the initiative from the terrorists and reimpose the rule of law on the Creggan and Bogside. Hooligan activity was to be vigorously countered and arrest operations were to be mounted. As a result, a series of operations was carried out in the Bogside and Creggan at battalion strength with the object of clearing barricades, making arrests and searching premises about which intelligence reports had been received. These operations hardened the attitude of the community against the Army, so that the troops were operating in an entirely hostile environment and as time went on were opposed by all elements of the community when they entered the Bogside and Creggan. The Army's static positions and observation posts were fired on and a large number of youths, many of them unemployed, gathered daily at the points of entry into the areas which were guarded by troops in order to attack them with stones and other missiles. Many nail and petrol bombs were thrown during these attacks. Gunmen made full use of the cover offered to them by the gangs of youths, which made it more and more difficult to engage the youths at close quarters and make arrests. The Creggan became almost a fortress. Whenever troops appeared near there at night search-lights were switched on and car horns blazed. The terrorists were still firmly in control.

Early in 1972 the security authorities were concerned that the violence was now spreading northwards from William Street, which was the line on the northern fringe of the Bogside on which the troops had for some considerable time taken their stand. Bombing and arson attacks on shops, offices and commercial premises were taking place with increasing frequency in Great James Street and Waterloo Place. The local traders feared that the whole of this shopping area would be extinguished within the next few months. A few figures will show the serious threat not only to the commercial areas of the City but also to the lives of the security forces. From 1 August 1971 to 9 February 1972 in Londonderry 2,656 shots were fired at the security forces, 456 nail and gelignite bombs were thrown and there were 225 explosions, mostly against business premises. In reply the security forces fired back 840 live rounds. In the last two weeks of January the IRA was particularly active. In 80 separate incidents in Londonderry 319 shots were fired at the security forces and 84 nail bombs were thrown at them; two men of the security forces were killed and two wounded. The Londonderry Development Commission has estimated that between 1 August 1971 and about the middle of February 1972 damage amounting to more than £6 million was inflicted in Londonderry. Since then there has been further heavy damage.

At the beginning of 1972 Army foot patrols were not able to operate south of William Street by day because of sniper fire, although the Army continued to patrol in the Bogside at night and to enter by day if there was a specific reason for so doing. There were no foot patrols by day during January. The hooligan gangs in Londonderry constituted a special threat to security. Their tactics were to engineer daily breaches of law and order in the face of the security forces, particularly in the William Street area, during which the lives of the soldiers were at risk from attendant snipers and nail bombers. The hooligans could be contained but not dispersed without serious risk to the troops.

This was the background against which it was learned that, despite the fact that parades and processions had been prohibited throughout Northern Ireland by law since 9 August 1971, there was to be a protest march in Londonderry on Sunday 30 January, organised by the Northern Ireland Civil Rights Association (NICRA). It was the opinion of the Army commanders that if the march took place, whatever the intentions of NICRA might be, the hooligans backed up by the gunmen would take control. In the light of this view the security forces made their plans to block the march.

THE ARMY PLAN TO CONTAIN THE MARCH

The proposed march placed the security forces in a dilemma. An attempt to stop by force a crowd of 5,000 or more, perhaps as many as 20 or 25,000, might result in heavy casualties or even in the over-running of the troops by sheer weight of numbers. To allow such a well publicised march to take place without opposition, however, would bring the law into disrepute and make control of future marches impossible.

Chief Superintendent Lagan, the head of the Royal Ulster Constabulary (RUC) in Londonderry, thought that the dangers of interfering with the march were too great and that no action should be taken against it save to photograph the leaders with a view to their being prosecuted later. His opinion was reported to the Chief Constable of Northern Ireland and to the Commander 8 Infantry Brigade (Brigadier MacLellan) who passed it to General Ford, the Commander Land Forces Northern Ireland. The final decision, which was taken by higher authority after General Ford and the Chief Constable had been consulted, was to allow the march to begin but to contain it within the general area of the Bogside and the Creggan Estate so as to prevent rioting in the City centre and damage to commercial premises and shops. On 25 January General Ford put the Commander 8 Infantry Brigade in charge of the operation and ordered him to prepare a detailed plan. The plan is 8 Infantry Brigade Operation Order No 2/72 dated 27 January.

The Brigade Commander's plan required the erection of barriers sealing off each of the streets through which the marchers might cross the containment line. Though there were 26 barriers in all, the Inquiry was concerned with only three:

No. 12 in Little James Street;

No. 13 in Sackville Street;

No. 14 in William Street.

The barriers, which were to consist of wooden knife rests reinforced with barbed wire and concrete slabs, were to be put in place early in the afternoon of 30 January. At some of them, notably at barrier 14, an armoured personnel carrier was placed on either side of the street close behind and almost parallel with the barrier to reinforce it and to give the troops some cover from stone throwing. Each barrier was to be manned by the Army in platoon strength with representative RUC officers in support. The troops at the barriers were to be provided by units normally under command of 8 Infantry Brigade. The following troops and equipment were to be brought in as reinforcements and reserves:

1st Battalion Parachute Regiment (hereafter referred to as 1 Para);

1st Battalion Kings Own Border Regiment;

2 Companies of the 3rd Battalion Royal Regiment of Fusiliers;

2 water cannon.

The Operation Order provided that the march should be dealt with in as low a key as possible for as long as possible and indeed that if it took place entirely within the Bogside and Creggan it should go unchallenged. No action was to be taken against the marchers unless they tried to breach the barriers or used violence against the security forces. CS gas was not to be used except as a last resort if troops were about to be overrun and the rioters could no longer be held off with water cannon and riot guns. (These guns, which fire rubber bullets, are also known as baton guns; and the rubber bullets as baton rounds.)

Under the heading of "Hooliganism" the Operation Order provided:

> An arrest force is to be held centrally behind
> the check points and launched in a scoop-up opera-
> tion to arrest as many hooligans and
> rioters as possible.

This links up with the specific task allotted to 1 Para which was in the following terms:

1. Maintain a Brigade Arrest Force to conduct a scoop-up operation of as many hooligans and rioters as possible.

(a)   This operation will only be launched either
in whole or in part on the orders
of the Brigade Commander.

(b) . . .

(c) . . .

(d)   It is expected that the arrest operation
will be conducted on foot.

2.   A secondary role of the force will be to
act as the second Brigade mobile reserve.

The Operation Order, which was classified
"Secret", thus clearly allotted to 1 Para the task of
an arrest operation against hooligans. Under cross-
examination, however, the senior Army officers,
and particularly General Ford, were severely
attacked on the grounds that they did not genuine-
ly intend to use 1 Para in this way. It was suggested
that 1 Para had been specially brought to
Londonderry because they were known to be the
roughest and toughest unit in Northern Ireland and
it was intended to use them in one of two ways:
either to flush out any IRA gunmen in the Bogside
and destroy them by superior training and fire
power; or to send a punitive force into the Bogside
to give the residents a rough handling and discour-
age them from making or supporting further attacks
on the troops.

There is not a shred of evidence to support these suggestions and they have been denied by all the officers concerned. I am satisfied that the Brigade Operation Order accurately expressed the Brigade Commander's intention for the employment of 1 Para and that suggestions to the contrary are unfounded. 1 Para was chosen for the arrest role because it was the only experienced uncommitted battalion in Northern Ireland. Other experienced units were stationed in Londonderry as part of the normal content of 8 Infantry Brigade, but being committed to barrier and other duties they were not available for use as an arrest force. The arrest operation was vigorously carried out. At the end of the afternoon 54 people had been arrested by 1 Para, about 30 of them by Support Company.

Another unjustified criticism of General Ford was persisted in throughout the Tribunal hearing. It was said that when heavy firing began and it became apparent that the operation had taken an unexpected course, the General made no attempt to discover the cause of the shooting but instead washed his hands of the affair and walked away. This criticism is based on a failure to understand the structure of command in the Army. The officer commanding the operation was the Commander 8 Brigade, who was in his Operations Room and was the only senior officer who had any general picture of what was going on. General Ford was present on the streets of Londonderry as an observer only. Although he had wireless equipment in his vehicle he was not accompanied by a wireless operator when on foot. When the serious shooting began the General was on foot in the neighbourhood of Chamberlain Street and had no means of knowing what was going on. Nothing would have been more likely to create chaos than for him to assume command or even to interfere with radio traffic by asking for information. Instead he did the only possible thing by going at once to an observation post from which he could observe the scene for himself.

THE MARCH AS IT HAPPENED

The marchers assembled on the Creggan Estate on a fine sunny afternoon and in carnival mood. At first amounting to some hundreds only they toured the estate collecting additional numbers as they went and eventually the total may have been something between 3,000 and 5,000 people. At their head was a lorry carrying a Civil Rights Association banner and travelling upon the lorry were some of the leaders of the march. The marchers did not move in any kind of military formation but walked as a crowd through the streets, occupying the entire width of

the road, both carriage-way way and pavements.
The marchers, who included many women and
some children, were orderly and in the main good
humoured. When in due course they appeared at
the west end of William Street it was obvious that
their direct route to the Guildhall Square lay along
William Street itself and that the march would come
face to face with the Army at barrier 14 in that street.
At this stage it became noticeable that a large number of youths, of what was described throughout the
Inquiry as the hooligan type, had placed themselves
at the head of the march; indeed some of them were
in front of the lorry itself. Some relatively minor
exchanges took place between these youths and the
soldiers manning the barriers which the march
passed on its way to William Street, but nothing of
real consequence occurred until the marchers
reached the barriers in Little James Street and
William Street. When the leaders of the march
reached the junction of William Street and Rossville
Street the lorry turned to its right to go along
Rossville Street and the stewards made strenuous
efforts to persuade the marchers to follow the lorry.
It is quite evident now that the leaders of the march
had decided before setting off from the Creggan
Estate that they would take this course and thus
avoid a head-on confrontation with the Army at the
William Street barrier.

However, this change of direction was not acceptable to a great many of the marchers. The stewards' attempts to divert the march were greeted with jeers and cat-calls. In the event although large numbers of non-violent marchers were persuaded to turn to their right into Rossville Street a substantial number, not all of them youths, continued into the cul-de-sac created by the William Street barrier. The television films made by the BBC and Independent Television News show graphically how this crowd approached to within touching distance of the barrier itself. The pressure of the crowd from behind was heavy and a densely packed mass formed at the barrier, which was manned by men of the Royal Green Jackets. The television films taken from behind the troops at the barrier show that the conduct of these soldiers was impeccable, despite the ugly situation which developed. The films show at least one middle-aged man making some attempt to move the barrier aside. Had other members of the crowd followed his example, the results might have been disastrous. A steward managed to divert this particular man from his intention. There is a very illuminating view in the television films of the packed crowd standing at the barrier spitting and shouting obscenities at the troops behind it. If the crowd had made up their minds to make their way through the barrier by sheer force grave injuries must have been suffered both by civilians and soldiers; but happily this point was never reached. After a time the movement of the crowd at the rear reduced the pressure on those at the front in William Street and the crowd in front of the barrier began to thin out somewhat. The hooligans at once took advantage of the opportunity to start stone-throwing on a very violent scale. Not only stones, but objects such as fire grates and metal rods used as lances were thrown violently at the troops in a most dangerous way. This scene was observed by millions on television on the night in question and I have myself seen it replayed on three occasions. Some witnesses have sought to play down this part of the incident and to suggest that it was nothing more than a little light stoning of the kind which occurs on most afternoons in this district and is accepted as customary. All I can say is that if this in any way represents normality the degree of violence to which the troops are normally subjected is very much greater than I suspect most people in Britain have appreciated. The troops responded with controlled volleys of rubber bullets but this was in some degree countered by the hooligans bringing forward an improvised shield of corrugated iron behind which they could shelter from the bullets. Accordingly a water cannon which had been held in reserve was brought up behind the barrier and proceeded to drench the hooligan crowd with water coloured with a purple dye. Unfortunately, from the soldiers' point of view, a canister of CS gas thrown by a member of the crowd happened to explode underneath the water cannon incommoding the crew who were not wearing their gas masks. The water cannon was therefore withdrawn for a few minutes and rubber bullets were fired again with little more effect than on the previous occasion. When the gas had cleared from the water cannon it was brought forward a second time and used upon the crowd to some effect. At about 1555 hours the troops appeared to be reaching a position in which they might disperse the rioters and relieve the pressure upon themselves. It was at this point that the decision to go ahead with the arrest operation, for which 1 Para was earmarked, was made.

THE LAUNCHING OF THE ARREST OPERATION

Since the tactics of the arrest operation were to be determined by the location and strength of the rioters at the time when it was launched, the Brigade Order left them to be decided by Lieutenant Colonel Wilford, Commanding Officer (CO) of 1 Para. He had three Companies available for the arrest operation: A Company, C Company and Support Company, the latter being reinforced by a Composite Platoon from Administrative Company. (A fourth Company had been detached and put under command of 22 Light Air Defence Regiment for duties elsewhere in Londonderry.) In the event these three Companies moved forward at the same time. A Company operated in the region of the Little Diamond and played no significant part in the events with which the Inquiry was concerned. C Company went forward on foot through barrier 14 and along Chamberlain Street, while Support Company drove in vehicles through barrier 12 into Rossville Street to encircle rioters on the waste ground or pursued by C Company along Chamberlain Street. The only Company of 1 Para to open fire that afternoon—other than with riot guns—was Support Company.

Before the wisdom of the order launching the arrest operation is considered it is necessary to decide who gave it. According to the Commander 8 Brigade and his Brigade Major (Lieutenant Colonel Steele) the operation was authorised by the Brigadier personally, as indeed was envisaged in the Brigade Order. The order for 1 Para to go in and make arrests was passed by the Brigade Major to the Commanding Officer 1 Para on a secure wireless link, i.e. one which was not open to eavesdropping.

This link was used because the arrest operation depended on surprise for its success and it was known that normal military wireless traffic was not secure. The Commanding Officer 1 Para confirmed that he received the order and all three officers agreed that the order was in terms which left the Commanding Officer free to employ all three Companies.

During the Inquiry, however, it was contended that the Brigadier did not authorise the arrest operation and that it was carried out by Lieutenant Colonel Wilford in defiance of orders or without orders and on his own initiative. The suspicion that Lieutenant Colonel Wilford acted without authority derives from the absence of any relevant order in the verbatim record of wireless traffic on the ordinary Brigade net. This omission was due to the use of the secure wireless link for this one vital order, as mentioned in the previous paragraph.

Other circumstances which suggest that 1 Para moved without orders are less easily explained. The Brigade log, which is maintained in the Brigade Operations Room and is a minute-by-minute record of events and messages, regardless of the method of communication used, contains the following entries:

Serial 147, 1555 hours from 1 Para. Would like to deploy sub-unit through barricade 14 to pick up yobbos in William Street/Little James Street.

Serial 159, 1609 hours from Brigade Major. Orders given to 1 Para at 1607 hours for one sub-unit of 1 Para to do scoop-up op through barrier 14. *Not* to conduct running battle down Rossville Street.

Serial 159 is identified by the Brigade Major as recording the Brigadier's instruction for 1 Para to move; but its terms are inconsistent with the employment of three Companies. (A sub-unit is a Company.) Further, the Brigade Operation Order said that it was expected that the arrest operation would be conducted on foot and that the two axes of advance were likely to be towards the areas of William Street/Little Diamond and William Street/Little James Street, i.e. the Order did not contemplate the use of Rossville Street as an axis of advance; and whatever the prohibition of a "running battle down Rossville Street" was intended to imply it at least suggests that a penetration in depth at this point was not intended. It has been contended that the Brigade log shows prima facie that the only action which 1 Para was authorised to carry out was the limited one for which permission had been sought in the message recorded in Serial 147. This view is supported by the evidence of Chief Superintendent Lagan, who was in the Brigadier's office at the relevant time and who formed the impression that 1 Para had acted without authority from the Brigadier.

It is understandable that these circumstances have given rise to suspicion that the CO 1 Para exceeded his orders, but I do not accept this conclusion in the face of the sworn evidence of the three officers concerned. I think that the most likely explanation is that when the Brigade Major gave instructions to the log keeper to make the entry which appears as Serial 159 the latter mistakenly thought that the order was a response to the request in Serial 147 and he entered it accordingly.

SHOULD THE ARREST OPERATION HAVE BEEN LAUNCHED AT ALL?

By 1600 hours the pressure on barrier 14 had relaxed. There were still 100 to 200 hooligans in the William Street area but most of the non-violent marchers had either turned for home or were making their way down Rossville Street to attend a meeting at Free Derry Corner where about 500 were already assembled. On the waste ground between the Rossville Flats and William Street there was a mixed crowd of perhaps 200 which included some rioters together with marchers, local residents, newspapermen and sightseers who were moving aimlessly about or chatting in groups. This was the situation when Commander 8 Brigade ordered 1 Para to move forward and make arrests.

In the light of events the wisdom of carrying out the arrest operation is debatable. The Army had achieved its main purpose of containing the march and although some rioters were still active in William Street they could have been dispersed without difficulty. It may well be that if the Army had maintained its "low key" attitude the rest of the day would have passed off without further serious incident. On the other hand the Army had been subjected to severe stoning for upwards of half an hour; and the future threat to law and order posed by the hard core of hooligans in Londonderry made the arrest of some of them a legitimate security objective. The presence of 1 Para provided just the opportunity to carry this out.

In view of the large numbers of people about in the area the arrest operation presented two particular risks: first, that in a large-scale scoop-up of rioters a number of people who were not rioters would be caught in the net and perhaps roughly handled; secondly, that if the troops were fired upon and returned fire innocent civilians might well be injured.

Commander 8 Brigade sought to minimise the first risk by withholding the order to launch the arrest operation until the rioters and the marchers were clearly separated. But this separation never really happened. At 1607 hours when 1 Para was ordered forward a substantial crowd remained on the waste ground between the bulk of the rioters who were in William Street and the bulk of the marchers who had either reached Free Derry Corner or gone home. The Brigade Commander, who could not see the area at all, relied mainly upon information from an officer in a helicopter, which information may have been incomplete. The Brigade Commander in giving evidence told me that he had considered the possibility that if a shooting match developed there would be risk to innocent people but he described this risk as "very bare". On the whole he considered that the arrest operation was essential in the interests of security and gave the order accordingly. Whether the Brigade Commander was guilty of an error of judgment in giving orders for the arrest operation to proceed is a question which others can judge as well or better than I can. It was a decision made in good faith by an experienced officer on the information available to him, but he underestimated the dangers involved.

THE FIRST HIGH-VELOCITY ROUNDS

Shortly before 1600 hours, and before the Paras had moved across William Street, two incidents occurred there involving the firing of high-velocity rounds. Although they are not of particular importance in the context of the afternoon as a whole, they are interesting if only because their circumstances can be ascertained with a fair degree of certainty. The officers of 1 Para had previously been engaged in the morning on reconnaissance of various routes that could be used if the Battalion were called upon to move forward and make arrests in the area of Rossville Street and William Street. Obviously the Battalion could move the barriers and go through them; but at one time it was thought that they might wish to enter William Street somewhat to the west of Little James Street in order to outflank the vacant land at "Aggro Corner" (the corner of William Street and Rossville Street). The Company Commander of the Support Company found a route over a wall by the side of the Presbyterian Church which he considered might be useful for this purpose, but which was obstructed by wire. Accordingly he sent a wire-cutting party to make this route usable if required. Whilst some soldiers from the Mortar Platoon were cutting the wire, a single high-velocity round was fired from somewhere near the Rossville Flats and struck a rainwater pipe on the side of the Presbyterian Church just above their heads. A large number of witnesses gave evidence about this incident, which clearly occurred, and which proves that at that stage there was at least one sniper, equipped with a high velocity weapon, established somewhere in the vicinity of the Rossville Flats and prepared to open fire on the soldiers.

The Company Commander of Support Company had sent a number of men forward to cover the wire-cutting party. Some of these men established themselves on the two lower floors of a three-storey derelict building on William Street, just to the west of some open land near the Presbyterian Church. They had not been there very long before their presence was noticed by some of the youths who were throwing stones in Little James Street, a substantial party of whom shifted their attention to the soldiers in the derelict building. A hail of missiles was thrown at these soldiers. After a time Soldier A fired two rounds and Soldier B fired three rounds. There is no doubt that this shooting wounded Mr John Johnson and Mr Damien Donaghy. Evidence from civilians in the neighbourhood, including Mr Johnson himself, is to the effect that although stones were being thrown no firearms or bombs were being used against the soldiers in the derelict building. Having seen and heard Mr Johnson I have no doubt that he was telling the truth as he saw it. He was obviously an innocent passer-by going about his own business in Londonderry that afternoon and was almost certainly shot by accident. I have not thought it necessary to take a statement from Mr Donaghy, who was injured more seriously and was still in hospital when I finished hearing evidence. I am quite satisfied that had he given evidence it would have been in the same sense as that given by Mr Johnson.

What, then, is the explanation of this incident from the Army side? Soldier A, a Corporal, described the incident as follows. He was on the middle floor of the building. From the window he saw some young men, who were hanging around after the main body of the march had passed, start throwing stones and bottles at the soldiers on the ground floor, some of whom replied with rubber bullets. He then saw two smoking objects, about the size of a bean can, go sailing past the window; and heard two explosions, louder than the explosion of the rubber-bullet guns. As the two smoking objects went past the window he shouted 'Nail bombs' as a warning to the men on the ground floor. His Platoon Sergeant called back an order that he was to shoot any nail bombers. He then saw, about 50 yards away on the other side of the road, a man look round the corner and dart back again. The man reappeared carrying an object in his right hand and made the actions of striking a fuse match against the wall with his left hand. When he brought his two hands together Soldier A assumed that he was about to light a nail bomb, took aim and fired at him. His first shot missed, so Soldier A fired again immediately and this time saw the man fall. Other people at once came out from the side of the building and dragged the man away.

Soldier B's description of the incident was in similar terms. He was on the ground floor of the building with his Platoon Sergeant and three other soldiers of the Platoon. A group of about 50 youths was throwing stones at them, undeterred by shots from the two baton guns which the soldiers had with them. Some of the stones came through the window space. He heard the explosion of two nail bombs on the waste ground to the left of the building, but did not see them in flight because he was putting on his gas mask at the time. He noticed one man come out from the waste ground across William Street carrying in his right hand a black cylindrical object which looked like a nail bomb. With his left hand he struck the wall with a match. Thinking that the man was about to light the nail bomb, and that there was no time to wait for orders from his Platoon Sergeant, Soldier B took aim and fired. As the first shot had no effect, he fired two more shots, whereupon the man fell back and was dragged away by two of his comrades. Under cross-examination Soldier B agreed that the wearing of a gas mask made it more difficult to take proper aim.

I find it impossible to reach any conclusion as to whether explosive substances were thrown at these soldiers or not. Mere negative evidence that nail bombs were not seen or heard is of relatively little importance in a situation in which there was already a great deal of noise. Baton rounds were being fired from the barrier in Little James Street nearby and there were other distractions for the various witnesses. Having seen Soldiers A and B vigorously cross-examined I accept that they thought, rightly or wrongly, that the missiles being thrown towards them included a nail bomb or bombs; and that they thought, rightly or wrongly, that one of the members of the crowd was engaged in suspicious action similar to that of striking a match and lighting a nail bomb. The soldiers fired in the belief that they were entitled to do so by their orders. Whether or not the circumstances were really such as to warrant firing there is no reason whatever to suppose that either Mr Johnson or Mr Donaghy was in fact trying to light or throw a bomb.

SUPPORT COMPANY IN ACTION

An ammunition check on return to barracks showed that Support Company of 1 Para had, in the course of 30 January, expended 108 rounds of 7.62 mm ammunition. This is the ammunition which is used in the SLR rifle, with which all ranks in the Company were armed, except three who had sub-machine guns. Some of the men carried, in addition to their SLR, a baton gun or baton. The only other weapon with which the Company was equipped that day was the Browning machine gun on a Ferret scout car. No Browning or sub-machine gun ammunition had been used. Five rounds of 7.62 mm ammunition had been fired by Soldiers A and B as already described above and one had been ejected unfired by a soldier in clearing a stoppage in his rifle. The remaining 102 rounds were fired by soldiers of Support Company in a period of under 30 minutes between 1610 and 1640 hours. About 20 more rounds were fired by the

Army in Londonderry that afternoon, but not by 1 Para and not in the area with which the Tribunal was primarily concerned.

Support Company advanced through barrier 12 and down Rossville Street in a convoy of 10 vehicles. A photograph taken very shortly afterwards shows the Guildhall clock standing at 10 minutes past 4. In the lead was the Mortar Platoon commanded by Lieutenant N, comprising 18 all ranks and travelling in two armoured personnel carriers (APCs, colloquially known to the Army as "Pigs"). Next came the Command APC of the Company Commander (Major 236) with a Ferret scout car in attendance. Following Company Headquarters came two empty APCs belonging to the Machine Gun Platoon. The men of this Platoon had been detached earlier and did not rejoin the Company in time to take part in the arrests. The two empty APCs were followed by two soft-skinned 4-ton lorries carrying the 36 all ranks of the Composite Platoon, commanded by Captain SA8. The rear was brought up by two further APCs carrying the Anti-Tank Platoon, which consisted of Lieutenant 119 in command and 17 other ranks.

According to Major 236 his orders were simply to go through barrier 12 and arrest as many rioters as possible. As the rioters retreated down Rossville Street he went after them.

The leading APC (Lieutenant N) turned left off Rossville Street and halted on the waste ground near to where Eden Place used to be. The second APC (Sergeant O) went somewhat further and halted in the courtyard of the Rossville Flats near the north end of the western (or No. 1) Block. The Platoon immediately dismounted. Soldier P and one or two others from Sergeant O's vehicle moved towards Rossville Street but the remainder of the Platoon started to make arrests near to their vehicles.

Meanwhile the remainder of Support Company vehicles had halted in Rossville Street. The Company Commander (Major 236) says that his command vehicle came under fire so he moved it with his scout car in attendance to the north end of No. 1 Block of Rossville Flats to obtain cover. The soft-skinned vehicles of the Composite Platoon halted under cover of buildings at the south-east corner of the junction of William Street and Rossville Street, where the troops dismounted. The Anti-Tank Platoon's vehicles halted behind the 4-ton lorries and the men of that Platoon dismounted and moved to Kells Walk. Some of these men were to appear later in Glenfada Park. The Composite

Platoon Commander deployed half of his men to the east in support of the Mortar Platoon, the other half to the west in support of the Anti-Tank Platoon.

Thereafter Support Company operated in three areas which require separate examination: the courtyard of the Rossville Flats; Rossville Street from Kells Walk to the improvised barricade; and lastly the area of Glenfada Park and Abbey Park.

The activities of Mortar Platoon in the courtyard of the Rossville Flats

As soon as the vehicles appeared in William Street the crowd on the waste ground began to run away to the south and was augmented by many other people driven out of Chamberlain Street by C Company. Some of the crowd ran along Rossville Street on the west side of Block 1 of the flats, whilst the remainder ran into the courtyard on the north side of the flats themselves. The crowd ran not because they thought the soldiers would open fire upon them but because they feared arrest. Though there was complete confidence that the soldiers would not fire unless fired upon, experienced citizens like Father Daly recognised that an arrest operation was in progress and wished to avoid the rubber bullets and rough handling which this might involve. One of the photographs taken by Mr Tucker from his home in the central block of the Rossville Flats shows clearly what was happening at this stage. However, careful study of the photograph shows that many of the crowd remained under cover in the doorways of the flats or remained facing the vehicles to see how far they would come.

The APCs of Mortar Platoon penetrated more deeply than was expected by the crowd, which caused some panic. The only means of escape from the courtyard was the alleyway between Blocks 1 and 2 and that between Blocks 2 and 3, both of which rapidly became very congested. As soon as the vehicles halted the soldiers of Mortar Platoon began to make arrests. But within a minute or two firing broke out and within about the next 10 minutes the soldiers of Mortar Platoon had fired 42 rounds of 7.62 mm ammunition and one casualty (John Duddy) lay dead in the courtyard.

This action in the courtyard is of special importance for two reasons. The first shots, other than those in William Street referred to previously, were fired here. Their sound must have caused other soldiers to believe that Support Company was under attack and made them more ready than they would otherwise have been to identify gunmen amongst the crowd.

Secondly, the shooting by the Mortar Platoon in the courtyard was one of the incidents invoked by those who have accused the Army of firing indiscriminately on the backs of a fleeing crowd.

I have heard a great deal of evidence from civilians, including pressmen, who were in the crowd in the courtyard, almost all to the effect that the troops did not come under attack but opened fire without provocation. The Army case is that as soon as they began to make arrests they themselves came under fire and their own shooting consisted of aimed shots at gunmen and bomb throwers who were attacking them. This issue, sometimes referred to as "Who fired first?", is probably the most important single issue which I have been required to determine.

Civilian evidence

A representative sample of the civilian evidence is as follows:

Father Daly was in the area out of concern for some elderly parishioners who lived there. Having seen the Army carry out arrest operations before on the waste ground he did not think that the vehicles would travel beyond Eden Place. He did not run away until he saw that they were coming further and he was accordingly at the back of the running crowd. He overtook John Duddy as he ran. He heard a shot and looking over his shoulder saw Duddy fall. He saw no weapon in Duddy's hands. Father Daly ran on and after a few yards he heard a "fusillade of gunfire", a "huge number" of shots which he recognised as live bullets; so he dived to the ground. He was convinced that all the shots came from behind and thought that the rest of the crowd also believed this to be the case. Apart from one civilian with a pistol he saw no weapon in other than Army hands. When asked if he had seen any shooting from the roof of the Rossville Flats he answered "I do not think that I am qualified really to say. I cannot say that I looked up there that evening. I certainly was not aware of the sound of anything come from there."

Mr Simon Winchester, a *Guardian* reporter, was walking across the open ground to the north of Rossville Flats when he met a crowd of people moving away from the William Street area towards Free Derry Corner. He decided to go with the crowd. A very short time later a number of armoured vehicles swept in along Rossville Street and the crowd started running. Some ran along Rossville Street towards Free Derry Corner, others towards the exits between the three blocks of the Rossville Flats.

Mr Winchester heard a number of shots, probably less than 10, coming from behind him. He dropped to the ground, as did everyone else. In the ensuing panic and confusion he saw an injured man, bleeding profusely from the leg. Mr Winchester did not see or hear any nail bombs or petrol bombs, nor see any weapons other than those carried by the Army. He did not hear firing other than that which he attributed to Army rifles until after he had made his way through to the south side of the Rossville Flats. He came away from the Bogside that day with the impression that he had seen soldiers fire needlessly into a huge crowd.

Mrs Mary Bonnor, who lives in the central block of the Rossville Flats, said that from her flat she saw a crowd running towards the Rossville Flats from William Street followed by two armoured vehicles. Some soldiers jumped out. One of them knelt down and pointed his gun; another, firing from the waist, shot a boy in the back. Mrs Bonnor said that she heard no shots until the soldiers shot the boy (John Duddy). That was the first shot she heard.

Mr Derrick Tucker, who is English by birth and has served in the Royal Navy and the Royal Air Force, also lives in the central block of the Rossville Flats. From his flat he saw people start to run and shout as the armoured vehicles drove up Rossville Street. Soldiers at once jumped out and adopted firing positions beside their vehicle. One of them started firing towards the landings of the flats in Rossville Street. Mr Tucker saw the shooting of John Duddy and of Michael Bridge, who was injured in the leg. He estimated that the interval between the soldiers getting out of their vehicles and starting to fire was between 30 seconds and two minutes. During that time he heard no explosions nor any firing directed at the soldiers. The only firing he heard was of gas canisters and rubber bullets at the junction of William Street and Rossville Street. He said that he felt sickened and degraded by the action of the British Army against unarmed civilians.

Mr Joseph Doherty, who lives in the Creggan, ran away when he saw the Army vehicles moving up Rossville Street. As he did so he saw some soldiers coming out of the end of Chamberlain Street. One of these soldiers fired a round into the ground in front of the crowd, so Mr Doherty ran towards the alleyway between the blocks of flats. Looking back he saw the same soldier in the same position fire an aimed shot at someone he could not see. The shot into the ground was the first shot of the day of which he was aware. He did not see shooting at any stage, or hear nail bombs at any time.

Mr Francis Dunne, a Londonderry schoolteacher, said that he was drifting across the open ground in front of the Rossville Flats towards Free Derry Corner. He was just short of Eden Place when the crowd on the open ground, which was very large, probably some hundreds, began to run. He ran too, as far as the north end of Block 1 of the Rossville Flats. From there he saw the armoured vehicles driving in. He made for the alleyway between Blocks 1 and 2 and found it jammed with people. Up to that stage he was not aware of any shots. He saw three soldiers along the back of the houses in Chamberlain Street and heard firing start. He saw the soldier at the front fire. Those three soldiers were not being molested, though some youths were throwing stones towards the end of Block 1. The front soldier fired at and hit a tall fair-haired young man. Mr Dunne saw that the alleyway through the flats was no longer jammed and went through it. His impression was that shots were coming through the alleyway towards him (i.e. from the direction of the soldiers) and he realised that live bullets were being fired. He was certain that there was no firing at the soldiers from the Rossville Flats as he ran across the courtyard towards the flats. Neither were there any nail bombs. He was convinced that as the soldiers came in and immediately afterwards there could not have been fire on them from the Rossville Flats without him knowing about it.

Army evidence

Evidence from the Army side about the shooting in the courtyard came from Major 236, Lieutenant N, Sergeant O and each of the soldiers who had fired in that area. Although the entire action took place in an area barely 100 yards square the general confusion appears to have been such that, like the civilian witnesses, soldiers spoke only to their immediate and personal experiences.

Major 236 halted his command vehicle in Rossville Street and said that as he and his driver dismounted a burst of about 15 rounds of low-velocity fire came towards them from the direction of Rossville Flats. They immediately moved the vehicle to a position at the north end of Block 1 in order to obtain cover from the shooting. There was, he said, continuous firing for the next 10 minutes. He saw seven or eight members of the Mortar Platoon firing aimed shots towards the flats but he could not see what they were firing at. He said that these soldiers were under fire.

Lieutenant N on leaving his vehicle was faced by a man throwing stones whom he tried to arrest but failed as the strap of his helmet broke. He then moved towards Chamberlain Street where he was faced by a hostile crowd and fired a total of three shots above their heads in order to disperse them. He then fired one further round at a man whom he thought was throwing a nail bomb in the direction of Sergeant O's vehicle. By this time the relevant firing in the courtyard was over and he had seen nothing of it.

Sergeant O, with 10 years' experience in the Parachute Regiment, had returned from a training course in Cyprus that very morning. When his vehicle halted he said that he and his men began to make arrests but were met with fire from the Rossville Flats. He thought that the fire came from four or five sources and possibly included some high-velocity weapons. He saw the strike of bullets four or five metres from one of the members of his Platoon. He and his men returned to his APC to secure their prisoners and then spread out in firing positions to engage those who had fired upon them. Sergeant O fired three rounds at a man firing a pistol from behind a car parked in the courtyard. The man fell and was carried away. He fired a further three rounds at a man standing at first-floor level on the cat-walk connecting Blocks 2 and 3, who was firing a fairly short weapon like an M1 carbine. The flashes at the muzzle were visible. Sergeant O caught a glimpse of Soldier S firing at a man with a similar weapon but his view was obscured by people "milling about". The Sergeant returned to his vehicle, but later fired two more rounds at a man whom he said was firing an M1 carbine from an alleyway between Blocks 2 and 3. He later saw Soldier T splashed with acid and told him that if further acid bombs were thrown he should return fire. He heard Soldier T fire two rounds and saw another acid bomb which had fallen. Sergeant O described the firing from the flats as the most intense that he had seen in Northern Ireland in such a short space of time.

Private Q, after dismounting from his vehicle, was being stoned and so took cover at the end of Block 1 of the Rossville Flats. There he heard four or five low-velocity shots, that is to say shots fired by someone other than the Army, though he could not say from what direction. Shortly afterwards he saw a man throwing nail bombs, two of which simply rolled away whilst another one exploded near to the houses backing on to Chamberlain Street. He shot at and hit the man as he was in the act of throwing another nail bomb. That bomb did not explode and the man's body was dragged away.

Private R heard one or two explosions like small bombs from the back of Rossville Flats. He also heard firing of high- and low-calibre weapons. He noticed a man about 30 yards along the eastern side of Block 1, who made as if to throw a smoking object, whereupon Private R fired at him. He thought he hit him high up on the shoulder, but was not certain what happened to the man because he was at that moment himself struck on the leg by an acid bomb thrown from an upper window in the flats. A few moments later R saw a hand firing a pistol from the alleyway between Blocks 2 and 3. R fired three times, but did not know whether he made a hit.

Private S said that he came under fire as soon as he dismounted from his vehicle. The fire was fairly rapid single shots, from the area of the Rossville Flats. He dodged across to the back of one of the houses in Chamberlain Street, from which position he saw a hail of bottles coming down from the flats on to one of the armoured vehicles and the soldiers around it. He fired a total of 12 shots at a gunman or gunmen who appeared, or reappeared, in front of the alleyway between Blocks 1 and 2 of the flats. The gunman was firing what he thought was an M1 carbine. He thought that he scored two hits.

Private T heard a burst of fire, possibly from a semi-automatic rifle being fired very quickly, about 30 to 45 seconds after dismounting from his vehicle. It came from somewhere inside the area of the Rossville Flats. He was splashed on the legs by acid from an acid bomb and noticed a person throwing acid bombs about three storeys up in the flats. On the orders of his Sergeant he fired two rounds at the acid-bomb thrower. He thought that he did not score a hit.

Lance Corporal V heard two explosions, not baton rounds or rifle fire, before his vehicle stopped. As soon as he jumped out he heard rifle fire and saw several shots spurting into the ground to his right. He thought that this fire was coming from the alley-way between Blocks 1 and 2 of the Rossville Flats. He saw a crowd of about 100 towards the end of Chamberlain Street who were throwing stones and bricks. Corporal V moved further forward and shot at and hit a man about 50 or 60 yards away from him in the act of throwing a bottle with a fuse attached to it.

A number of soldiers other than those of 1 Para gave evidence about the opening of fire. Captain 028, a Royal Artillery officer attached to 1 Para as a press officer, saw the leading vehicle struck by a round before it came to a halt and saw a man open fire with a sub-machine gun from the barricade as the soldiers jumped out of their vehicles. A few minutes later, during the gun battle, he saw a man armed with a pistol come out from the south end of Block 1 of the Rossville Flats, and another man with a rifle at a window in the flats. Lieutenant 227 of the Royal Artillery, who was in command of an observation post on the City Walls, heard two bursts of automatic fire from the Glenfada Park area after the arrest operation had begun and before he had heard any other sort of ball ammunition. He subsequently heard three or four pistol shots from the Rossville Flats area. Gunner 030, who was in a slightly different position on the City Walls, saw a youth fire five or six shots with a pistol from the south-east corner of the Rossville Flats courtyard in the direction of Rossville Street. This was before Gunner 030 heard any fire from the Paras. Later on he heard a burst of automatic fire and saw a man with a machine gun running in Glenfada Park.

There was also a considerable body of civilian evidence about the presence of gunmen in the Bogside that afternoon, including some to the effect that they were the first to open fire. Father Daly saw a man armed with a pistol fire two or three shots at the soldiers from the south end of Chamberlain Street.

Mr Dunne saw the same gunman. Father O'Gara saw a youth armed with a pistol fire three shots at the soldiers from Kells Walk. Both these episodes took place after the soldiers had opened fire. Mr Donnelly, a photographer of the Dublin newspaper the *Irish Times*, heard a single revolver shot in William Street 20 minutes before the Paras appeared on the scene; and Mr Capper, a BBC reporter, heard a single revolver shot fired from the crowd he was with at Kells Walk in the direction of soldiers in William Street. He heard this shot after the shooting of Mr Johnson and Mr Donaghy in William Street, but before the Paras moved into Rossville Street. Mr Beggin, a BBC cameraman, who went through the William Street barrier with soldiers of C Company and watched the soldiers of Support Company crossing the open ground in front of the Rossville Flats, heard a number of shots fired apparently from the flats before the soldiers themselves opened fire. Mr Phillips, Mr Seymour, Mr Wilkinson and Mr Hammond, members of an Independent Television News (ITN) team, who also went through the William Street barrier behind the Paras, all heard machine gun fire as the soldiers went across the open space. They also heard single shots but were not unanimous as to whether or not the automatic fire came first. It has been established that the troops did not use automatic weapons. So though the ITN men were not able to throw much light on the question of who fired first, their evidence did add considerable weight to the probability that the soldiers were fired on very soon after getting out of their vehicles. After the initial firing at the Rossville Street barricade, Mr Mailey, a resident of Londonderry and a free-lance photographer, heard three shots of a much lower calibre than that of the Army's weapons. Mr Winchester of the *Guardian* heard a single rifle shot from the direction of the Little Diamond some time before the Paras came through the barriers. A few minutes later and still before the Paras appeared, he saw youths clearing people away from an entrance to Columbcille Court in a manner which suggested to him that they were clearing a field of fire for a sniper. After he had reached the south side of the Rossville Flats he heard some low-calibre fire in answer to the Army's fire and also some automatic fire from the general direction of the flats. Mr Winchester and Mr Wade of the *Daily Telegraph* were fired at by a gunman armed with a low-calibre weapon, possibly a .22 rifle, as they made their way out of the Bogside at the end of the afternoon after the main shooting was over. Mr Bedell, a Londoner who was on holiday in Northern Ireland, was present at the meeting at Free Derry Corner. From there he saw the armoured vehicles arrive in Rossville Street and heard firing.

Some minutes later he saw several cars drive down from the Creggan. About two dozen men armed with rifles and automatic weapons got out, dispersed amongst the flats on the north side of Westland Street and fired about 50 rounds at the soldiers. When the gunmen withdrew, Mr Bedell saw a crowd of about 50 civilians surround and give cover to one of the gunmen who had been separated from the main body, so that he was able to rejoin the others in safety. Mr Kunioka, a Japanese student at the London Film School, saw a man armed with a rifle in Westland Street.

To those who seek to apportion responsibility for the events of 30 January the question "Who fired first?" is vital. I am entirely satisfied that the first firing in the courtyard was directed at the soldiers. Such a conclusion is not reached by counting heads or by selecting one particular witness as truthful in preference to another. It is a conclusion gradually built up over many days of listening to evidence and watching the demeanour of witnesses under cross-examination. It does not mean that witnesses who spoke in the opposite sense were not doing their best to be truthful. On the contrary I was much impressed by the care with which many of them, particularly the newspaper reporters, television men and photographers, gave evidence.

Notwithstanding the opinion of Sergeant O I do not think that the initial firing from the flats was particularly heavy and much of it may have been ill-directed fire from pistols and like weapons. The soldiers' response was immediate and members of the crowd running away in fear at the soldiers' presence understandably might fail to appreciate that the initial bursts had come from the direction of the flats. The photographs already referred to confirm that the soldiers' initial action was to make arrests and there was no reason why they should have suddenly desisted and begun to shoot unless they had come under fire themselves. If the soldiers are wrong they were parties in a lying conspiracy which must have come to light in the rigorous cross-examination to which they were subjected.

The action in Rossville Street

When the vehicle convoy halted in Rossville Street the Anti-Tank Platoon and one half of the Composite Platoon deployed to their right in the vicinity of the flats known as Kells Walk. From this point it is possible to look due south down Rossville Street to the rubble barricade in that street and beyond it to Free Derry Corner. The distance from Kells Walk to Free Derry Corner would be of the order of 300 yards. A considerable number of rounds was fired from Kells Walk in the direction of the barricade, at which at least four of the fatal casualties occurred.

It will be remembered that when the vehicles entered Rossville Street a densely packed crowd of perhaps 500 people was already assembled round the speakers' platform at Free Derry Corner and that the arrival of the soldiers caused some of the crowd on the waste ground also to run towards Free Derry Corner.

The barricade in Rossville Street running across from Glenfada Park to Block 1 of the Rossville Flats had fallen into disrepair and was only about three feet high. There was a gap to allow a single line of traffic to go through but there were also reinforcements of barbed wire on wooden knife rests. Although it would present no great obstacle to an athletic young man it would be a significant one to a crowd of people fleeing in panic down Rossville Street. Perhaps the most ugly of all the allegations made against the Army is that the soldiers at Kells Walk fired indiscriminately on a large and panic-stricken crowd which was seeking to escape over the barricade. The principal witness to support this allegation was Mr James Chapman, a civil servant who had previously been a regular

soldier in the British Army with the rank of
Warrant Officer Class 1. He had been a resident of
Londonderry for 36 years, 30 of them in the
Bogside itself. He lived at No. 6 Glenfada Park, so
that his sitting room window directly overlooked
the Rossville Street barricade. He described how
the main crowd of marchers, which he estimated at
5 to 6,000, had passed peacefully down Rossville
Street before the soldiers' vehicles appeared. When
the armoured personnel carriers appeared and the
rest of the crowd began to run some 50 to 100 soldiers deployed from their vehicles and, according
to Mr Chapman, immediately opened fire into
the crowd trying to flee over the barricade. Mr
Chapman is reported as having said in a television
interview on 3 February:

> I watched them shooting indiscriminately into a
> fleeing crowd of several thousand people, not just
> as some people say a few hundred hooligans.

In fairness to Mr Chapman there may have been
some confusion here and at the Inquiry his estimate
of the crowd crossing the barricade was of the order
of 200 to 300. He maintained, however, that the
Army fired indiscriminately upon the backs of that
number of people who were scrambling over the
barricade in an effort to escape and that no firearms

or bombs were being used against the soldiers at that time.

Mr Robert Campbell, the Assistant Chief Constable of the Renfrew and Bute Constabulary, who was observing the scene from the City Wall, gave a very different account of events at the barricade. He could not see the entry of the vehicles but he had a clear view of part of the barricade in Rossville Street and of the whole of the area to the south of it down to Free Derry Corner. He described how people streamed through the barricade on their way to the meeting at Free Derry Corner, but he also observed a group of demonstrators who detached themselves from the main crowd and remained close to the barricade from which they threw stones and other missiles in the direction of the Army vehicles. Mr Campbell described their stone-throwing as very active. After a time he heard automatic fire from the direction of the Rossville Flats. As this did not deter the stone-throwers he assumed that the rounds did not go near them. The automatic fire was followed by a single high-velocity shot which caused them to take cover. Within two or three minutes, however, the militants were throwing stones again. Then came a cluster of 10 or 12 high-velocity rounds which finally scattered them, leaving three or four bodies lying at the barricade.

Father O'Keefe, a lecturer in philosophy at the University of Ulster in Coleraine, gave a version of this incident which supported Mr Campbell rather than Mr Chapman. He said that when the armoured personnel carriers arrived, the bulk of the marchers had already moved to Free Derry Corner. He held back to make contact with friends and when the soldiers arrived he was part of a group of 25 to 30 people standing near the Rossville Street barricade. Whilst he and others took cover behind the gable end of the Glenfada Park flats, some five or six remained at the barricade and he had the impression that stones were being thrown. He said that the soldiers opened fire on the people at the barricade and he saw one of them hit and three bodies on the ground. At the end of his evidence I put Mr Chapman's account to him:

Q. One witness has told me that when the
soldiers fired and hit the three young men
standing at the barricade of whom you speak
at that time 100 or 150 people were trying
to make their way over and through the
barricade in order to get to Free Derry Corner
and that the three who were shot were shot
as they were endeavouring to climb over the
barricade. I take it that that is not the picture
as you saw it?

A. That is not the picture I have at all.

Mr Ronald Wood, an English-born citizen of Londonderry, who had served in the Royal Navy, also spoke of 30 to 40 people near the barricade, some of whom were throwing stones. Mr Donnelly, an *Irish Times* photographer, spoke of a thin line of about 20 youths and men behind the barricade. Further, the pathologist's evidence about the four young men who were casualties at the barricade, namely Kelly, Young, Nash and McDaid, was that they were not shot from behind.

I am entirely satisfied that when the soldiers first fired at the barricade they did not do so on the backs of a fleeing crowd but at a time when some 30 people, many of whom were young men who were or had been throwing missiles, were standing in the vicinity of the barricade.

It was not alleged that the shots fired in Glenfada Park, which are dealt with below, constituted firing on the backs of a fleeing crowd. But it was alleged that the crowd at Free Derry Corner was so fired on. What really happened at Free Derry Corner is clear because the evidence is almost all one way. If the line of fire from Kells Walk to the Rossville Street barricade is projected southward it comes dangerously close to Free Derry Corner. When the soldiers began to fire at the barricade the crowd around the speakers' platform, though agitated by the sound of the shooting, did not immediately break up. A second burst, however, caused the crowd to fall flat on their faces and at the next lull in the firing they quickly dispersed. There is no evidence that any soldier deliberately fired at this crowd. Lord Brockway, who was attempting to address the meeting at the time, acknowledged as much. No one in this crowd was injured, though some of the shots aimed at the barricade which missed their mark may have come uncomfortably close.

RESPONSIBILITY

Having dealt with the allegations of a general character made against the conduct of 1 Para on 30 January, I turn to consider the conduct of the individual soldiers who fired and the circumstances in which the individual civilians were killed.

The starting point of this part of the Inquiry is that 108 rounds of 7.62 mm ammunition were expended by members of Support Company. The Browning gun on the Company Commander's scout car was not fired nor were the three sub-machine guns. No shots were fired by the other Companies of 1 Para. I have no means of deciding which soldiers fired or how many rounds each fired except the evidence of the soldiers themselves. According to that evidence the allocation is as given in the table opposite.

The Army case is that each of these shots was an aimed shot fired at a civilian holding or using a bomb or firearm. On the other side it was argued that none of the deceased was using a bomb or firearm and that the soldiers fired without justification and either deliberately or recklessly.

To solve this conflict it is necessary to identify the particular shot which killed each deceased and the soldier who fired it. It is then necessary to consider the justification put forward by the soldier for firing and whether the deceased was in fact using a firearm or bomb. It has proved impossible to reach conclusions with this degree of particularity. In two instances a bullet was recovered from the body, so that the rifle, and thus the firer, was positively identified. But several shots fired by the same rifle cannot be distinguished

	Rounds	
Corporal A	2	
Private B	3	
Private C	5	
L/Corporal D	2	
Corporal E	3	
L/Corporal F	13	
Private G	6	
Private H	22	
L/Corporal J	2	
Sergeant K	1	
Private L	4	
Private M	2	
Lieutenant N	5	(4 plus 1 ejected unfired)
Sergeant O	8	
Corporal P	9	
Private Q	1	
Private R	4	
Private S	12	
Private T	2	
Private U	1	
L/Corporal V	1	
Total	108	

from one another and there is no certainty that a bullet hit the person at which it was aimed and whose conduct had caused the soldier to fire.

Another difficulty is that there is no certainty that the known casualty list is exhaustive. According to the Army evidence at least 25 civilians were hit, possibly more, of whom five or six were hit whilst firing from buildings or doorways. The Army's estimate of the number hit corresponds closely to the total number of known dead and wounded. But all the known dead, and all the wounded who gave evidence or about whom evidence was given, were hit in the open. Furthermore, some of those whom the Paras were confident they hit (e.g. the man hit by Sergeant O behind the Cortina car in the forecourt of the Rossville Flats) cannot be identified with any of the known dead or wounded. In addition, soldiers of the Royal Anglian Regiment and the Royal Artillery believe that they hit six or seven gunmen on whom they returned fire in other parts of Londonderry on 30 January; and nothing more is known about these casualties. There is a widely held belief that on some previous occasions when shots have been exchanged in Londonderry, casualties amongst the IRA and their supporters have been spirited away over the border into the Republic. Even a remote possibility that this occurred on

30 January increases the difficulty of trying to match a soldier's account of why he fired with other evidence of the conduct of an individual deceased.

WERE THE DECEASED CARRYING FIREARMS OR BOMBS?

Mr Campbell, the Scottish police officer, and a substantial number of soldiers gave evidence that they heard nail bombs exploding. The civilians were at one in denying that there were any such explosions. I did not conclude that some of the witnesses were necessarily lying on this point. Soldiers under attack, or expecting to be attacked, might well be quick to identify as nail bombs bangs otherwise unexplained. Conversely the civilians, hearing bangs at a time of confusion and panic and to the accompaniment of shouts and other loud noises, might be just as quick to attribute the bangs to the Army. Although a number of soldiers spoke of actually seeing firearms or bombs in the hands of civilians, none was recovered by the Army. None of the many photographs shows a civilian holding an object that can with certainty be identified as a firearm or bomb. No casualties were suffered by the soldiers from firearms or gelignite bombs. In relation to every one of the deceased there were eye witnesses who said that they saw no bomb or firearm in his hands. The clothing of 11 of the deceased when examined for explosive residues showed no trace of gelignite. The two others were Gerald McKinney, whose clothing had been washed at the hospital and could not be tested, and Donaghy, in the pockets of whose clothing there had, on any view, been nail bombs and whose case is considered later.

The only other relevant forensic test applied to the deceased was the so-called paraffin test. When a firearm is discharged minute particles of lead are carried by the propellant gases. The particles carried forward through the muzzle may be deposited over a distance of 30 feet in front of the weapon. Some gases escape from the breach however, and deposit lead particles on the hands or clothing of the firer. This phenomenon is particularly marked with revolvers and automatic weapons and with bolt-action rifles if the bolt is withdrawn after firing. If swabs are taken from the firing hand of a man who has fired such a weapon they may be expected to show an even distribution of minute lead particles on the back of that hand and between the forefinger and thumb. Such a deposit, if not otherwise explained, is strong if not conclusive evidence of firing.

Before such a conclusion is accepted, other possible

sources of the lead contamination must be examined. Amongst these are:

(a)   being close to someone else who is firing;

(b)   being within 30 feet of the muzzle of the weapon fired in one's own direction;

(c)   physical transfer of lead particles on contact with the body or clothing of someone who has recently fired a weapon;

(d)   the passing at close range of a bullet which has been damaged by contact with a hard substance and which may spread lead particles from its damaged surface;

(e)   direct contact with lead in, say, the trade of a plumber or whilst loading a firearm.

In deciding whether lead found on a subject's hand or clothing should be attributed to his having fired a weapon or to some other cause, much depends upon the pattern of the deposit itself. The characteristic of lead deposit from a weapon is an even distribution of minute particles, whereas the deposit from the handling of a body or object contaminated with lead is more likely to be in the form of a smear. According to the expert evidence of Dr Martin of the Northern Ireland Department of Industrial and Forensic Science and Professor Keith Simpson, a concentration of minute particles on the hand creates a "strong suspicion" that the subject has been firing.

The deceased considered individually

John Francis Duddy

Age 17. He was probably the first fatal casualty and fell in the courtyard of Rossville Flats. As already recounted, he was seen to fall by Father Daly. Mrs Bonnor and Mrs Duffy both spoke of seeing a soldier fire at him. According to Mrs Bonnor he was shot in the back. In fact the bullet entered his right shoulder and travelled through his body from right to left. As he ran he turned from time to time to watch the soldiers. This fits in with Father Daly having overtaken him while running and explains the entry wound being in his side. No shot described by a soldier precisely fits Duddy's case. The nearest is one described by Soldier V who spoke of firing at a man in a white shirt in the act of throwing a petrol bomb, but Duddy was wearing a red shirt and there is no evidence of his having a bomb. His reaction to the paraffin test was negative. I accept that Duddy was not carrying a bomb or firearm. The probable explanation of his death is that he was hit by a bullet intended for someone else.

Patrick Joseph Doherty

Age 31. His body was found in the area at the rear of No. 2 Block of Rossville Flats between that block and Joseph Place. His last moments are depicted in a remarkable series of photographs taken by Mr Peress which show him with a handkerchief over the lower part of his face crawling with others near the alleyway which separates No. 2 Block from No. 3. He was certainly hit from behind whilst crawling or crouching because the bullet entered his buttock and proceeded through his body almost parallel to the spine. There is some doubt as to whether he was shot when in the alleyway or at the point where his body was found. On the whole I prefer the latter conclusion. If this is so the probability is that he was shot by Soldier F, who spoke of hearing pistol shots and seeing a crouching man firing a pistol from the position where Doherty's body was found. Soldier F said that he fired as the man turned away, which would account for an entry wound in the buttock. Doherty's reaction to the paraffin test was negative. In the light of all the evidence I conclude that he was not carrying a weapon. If Soldier F shot Doherty in the belief that he had a pistol that belief was mistaken.

Hugh Pius Gilmore

Age 17. Gilmore died near the telephone box which stands south of Rossville Flats and near the alleyway separating Blocks 1 and 2. According to Miss Richmond he was one of a crowd of 30 to 50 people who ran away down Rossville Street when the soldiers appeared. She described his being hit just before he reached the barricade and told how she helped him to run on across the barricade towards the point where he collapsed. A photograph of Gilmore by Mr Robert White, which according to Miss Richmond was taken after he was hit, shows no weapon in his hand. The track of the bullet is not consistent with Gilmore being shot from directly behind and I think it likely that the statement of Mr Sean McDermott is more accurate on this point than the evidence of Miss Richmond. Mr McDermott put Gilmore as standing on the barricade in Rossville Street when he was hit and in a position such that his front or side may have been presented to the soldiers.

Gilmore was shot by one of the soldiers who fired from Kells Walk at the men at the barricade. It is impossible to identify the soldier. Gilmore's reaction to the paraffin test was negative. There is no evidence that he used a weapon.

Bernard McGuigan

Age 41. This man was shot within a short distance of Gilmore, on the south side of No. 2 Block of the Rossville Flats. According to Miss Richmond a wounded man was calling for help and Mr McGuigan, carrying a white handkerchief, deliberately left a position of cover to attend to him. She said that he was shot almost at once. Other civilian witnesses confirmed this evidence and photographs of McGuigan's body show the white handkerchief in question. Although there was some evidence that the shot came from Glenfada Park, which means that the soldier who fired might have been Soldier F, another possibility is that the shot came through the alleyway between Blocks 1 and 2. I cannot form any worthwhile conclusion on this point.

Although the eye witnesses all denied that McGuigan had a weapon, the paraffin test disclosed lead deposits on the right palm and the web, back and palm of his left hand. The deposit on the right hand was in the form of a smear, those on the left hand were similar to the deposits produced by a firearm. The earlier photographs of McGuigan's body show his head uncovered but in a later one it is covered with a scarf. The scarf showed a heavy deposit of lead, the distribution and density of which was consistent with the scarf having been used to wrap a revolver which had been fired several times. His widow was called to say that the scarf did not belong to him. I accept her evidence in concluding it is not possible to say that McGuigan was using or carrying a weapon at the time when he was shot. The paraffin test, however, constitutes ground for suspicion that he had been in close proximity to someone who had fired.

John Pius Young

Age 17. This young man was one of three who were shot at the Rossville Street barricade by one of the cluster of 10 to 12 shots referred to by Mr Campbell. Young is shown in Mr Mailey's photograph. Mr Mailey said that two men fell immediately after he took this photograph. Young was undoubtedly associated with the youths who were throwing missiles at the soldiers from the barricade and the track of the bullet suggests that he was facing the soldiers at the time. Several soldiers, notably P, J, U, C, K, L and M all said that they fired from the Kells Walk area at men who were using firearms or throwing missiles from the barricade. It is not possible to identify the particular soldier who shot Young.

The paraffin test disclosed lead particles on the web, back and palm of the left hand which were consistent with exposure to discharge gases from firearms. The body of Young, together with those of McDaid and Nash, was recovered from the barricade by soldiers of 1 Para and taken to hospital in an APC. It was contended at the hearing that the lead particles on Young's left hand might have been transferred from the hands of the soldiers who carried him or from the interior of the APC itself. Although these possibilities cannot be wholly excluded, the distribution of the particles seems to me to be more consistent with Young having discharged a firearm. When his case is considered in conjunction with those of Nash and McDaid and regard is had to the soldiers' evidence about civilians firing from the barricade, a very strong suspicion is raised that one or more of Young, Nash and McDaid was using a firearm. No weapon was found but there was sufficient opportunity for this to be removed by others.

Michael McDaid

Age 20. This man was shot when close to Young at the Rossville Street barricade. The bullet struck him in the front in the left cheek. The paraffin test disclosed abnormal lead particle density on his jacket and one large particle of lead on the back of the right hand. Any of the soldiers considered in connection with the death of Young might equally well have shot McDaid. Dr Martin thought that the lead density was consistent with McDaid having handled a firearm, but I think it more consistent with his having been in close proximity to someone firing.

William Noel Nash

Age 19. He also was close to Young and McDaid at the Rossville Street barricade and the three men were shot almost simultaneously. The bullet entered his chest from the front and particles of lead were detected on the web, back and palm of his left hand with a distribution consistent with his having used a firearm. Soldier P spoke of seeing a man firing a pistol from the barricade and said that he fired four shots at this man, one of which hit him in the chest. He thought that the pistol was removed by other civilians. In view of the site of the injury it is possible that Soldier P has given an accurate account of the death of Nash.

Mr Alexander Nash, father of William Nash, was wounded at the barricade. From a position of cover he saw that his son had been hit and went to help him. As he did so he himself was hit in the left arm. The medical opinion was that the bullet came from a low-velocity weapon and Soldier U described seeing Mr Nash senior hit by a revolver shot fired from the entrance to the Rossville Flats. The soldier saw no more than the weapon and the hand holding it. I think that the most probable explanation of this injury is that it was inflicted by a civilian firing haphazardly in the general direction of the soldiers without exposing himself enough to take proper aim.

Michael Kelly

Age 17. Kelly was shot while standing at the Rossville Street barricade in circumstances similar to those already described in the cases of Young, Nash and McDaid. The bullet entered his abdomen from the front which disposes of a suggestion in the evidence that he was running away at the time. The bullet was recovered and proved that Kelly was shot by Soldier F, who described having fired one shot from the Kells Walk area at a man at the barricade who was attempting to throw what appeared to be a nail bomb.

The lead particle density on Kelly's right cuff was above normal and was, I think, consistent with his having been close to someone using a firearm. This lends further support to the view that someone was firing at the soldiers from the barricade, but I do not think that this was Kelly nor am I satisfied that he was throwing a bomb at the time when he was shot.

Kevin McElhinney

Age 17. He was shot whilst crawling southwards along the pavement on the west side of No. 1 Block of Rossville Flats at a point between the barricade and the entrance to the flats. The bullet entered his buttock so that it is clear that he was shot from behind by a soldier in the area of Kells Walk. Lead particles were detected on the back of the left hand and the quantity of particles on the back of his jacket was significantly above normal, but this may have been due to the fact that the bullet had been damaged. Dr Martin thought the lead test inconclusive on this account. Although McElhinney may have been hit by any of the rounds fired from Kells Walk in the direction of the barricade—e.g. by Soldiers L and M—it seems probable that the firer was Sergeant K. This senior NCO was a qualified marksman whose rifle was fitted with a telescopic sight and who fired only one round in the course of the afternoon. He described two men crawling from the barricade in the direction of the door of the flats and said that the rear man was carrying a rifle. He fired one aimed shot but could not say whether it hit. Sergeant K obviously acted with responsibility and restraint. Though I hesitate to make a positive finding against a deceased man, I was much impressed by Sergeant K's evidence.

James Joseph Wray, Gerald McKinney, Gerald Donaghy and William McKinney

These four men were all shot somewhere near the south-west corner of the more northerly of the two courtyards of the flats at Glenfada Park. Their respective ages were 22, 35, 17 and 26. The two McKinneys were not related. Three other men wounded in the same area were Quinn, O'Donnell and Friel. I deal with the cases of these four deceased together because I find the evidence too confused and too contradictory to make separate consideration possible. One important respect in which the shooting in Glenfada Park differs from that at the Rossville Street barricade and in the forecourt of the Rossville Flats is that there is no photographic evidence.

Four soldiers, all from the Anti-Tank Platoon, fired in this area, namely E, F, G and H. Initially the Platoon deployed in the Kells Walk area and was involved in the firing at the Rossville Street barricade. It will be remembered that at this time some 30 or 40 people were in the region of the barricade, of whom some were engaging the soldiers whilst others were taking cover behind the nearby gable end of the flats in Glenfada Park. Corporal E described how he saw civilians firing from the barricade and then noticed some people move towards the courtyard of Glenfada Park. He said that on his own initiative he accordingly led a small group of soldiers into the courtyard from the north-east corner to cut these people off. The recollection of the Platoon Commander (Lieutenant 119) was somewhat different; he said that he sent Soldiers E and F into the courtyard of Glenfada Park to cut off a particular gunman who had been firing from the barricade. The result in any event was that Soldiers E and F advanced into the courtyard and Soldiers G and H followed shortly afterwards. In the next few minutes there was a very confused scene in which according to civilian evidence some of the people who had been sheltering near the gable end of Glenfada Park sought to escape by running through the courtyard in the direction of Abbey Park and the soldiers fired upon them killing the four men named at the head of this paragraph. Soldiers E, F and G gave an account of having been attacked by the civilians in this group and having fired in reply. Soldier H gave an account of his activities with which I deal later. From the forensic evidence about a bullet recovered from the body it is known that Soldier G shot Donaghy. It is clear that the other three were shot by Soldiers E, F, G or H. Although several witnesses spoke of having seen the bodies, there was a conflict of evidence as to whether they fell in the courtyard of Glenfada Park or between Glenfada Park and Abbey Park. The incident ended when the 20 to 30 civilians remaining in the courtyard were arrested on the orders of the Platoon Commander, who came into Glenfada Park just as the shooting finished.

In the face of such confused and conflicting testimony it is difficult to reach firm conclusions but it seems to me more probable that the civilians in Glenfada Park were running away than that they were seeking a battle with the soldiers in such a confined space. It may well be that some of them had been attacking the soldiers from the barricade, a possibility somewhat strengthened by the forensic evidence. The paraffin tests on the hand swabs and clothing of Gerald McKinney and William McKinney were negative. Dr Martin did not regard the result of the tests on Donaghy as positive but Professor Simpson did. The two experts agreed that the results of the tests on Wray were consistent with his having used a firearm. However, the balance of probability suggests that at the time when these four men were shot the group of civilians was not acting aggressively and that the shots were fired without justification. I am fortified in this view by the account given by Soldier H, who spoke of seeing a rifleman firing from a window of a flat on the south side of the Glenfada Park courtyard. Soldier H said that he fired an aimed shot at the man, who withdrew but returned a few moments later, whereupon Soldier H fired again. This process was repeated until Soldier H had fired 19 shots, with a break for a change of magazine. It is highly improbable that this cycle of events should repeat itself 19 times; and indeed it did not. I accepted evidence subsequently given, supported by photographs, which showed that no shot at all had been fired through the window in question. So 19 of the 22 shots fired by Soldier H were wholly unaccounted for.

A special feature of Gerald Donaghy's case has some relevance to his activities in the course of the afternoon although it does not directly bear on the circumstances in which he was shot.

After Donaghy fell he was taken into the house of Mr Raymond Rogan at 10 Abbey Park. He had been shot in the abdomen. He was wearing a blue denim blouse and trousers with pockets of the kind that open to the front rather than to the side. The evidence was that some at least of his pockets were examined for evidence of his identity and that his body was examined by Dr Kevin Swords, who normally worked in a hospital in Lincoln. Dr Swords' opinion was that Donaghy was alive but should go to hospital immediately. Mr Rogan volunteered to drive him there in his car. Mr Leo Young went with him to help. The car was stopped at a military check-point in Barrack Street, where Mr Rogan and Mr Young were made to get out. The car was then driven by a soldier to the Regimental Aid Post of 1st Battalion Royal Anglian Regiment, where Donaghy was examined by the Medical Officer (Soldier 138) who pronounced him dead. The

Medical Officer made a more detailed examination shortly afterwards but on neither occasion did he notice anything unusual in Donaghy's pockets. After another short interval, and whilst Donaghy's body still lay on the back seat of Mr Rogan's car, it was noticed that he had a nail bomb in one of his trouser pockets. An Ammunition Technical Officer (Bomb Disposal Officer, Soldier 127) was sent for and found four nail bombs in Donaghy's pockets.

There are two possible explanations of this evidence. First, that the bombs had been in Donaghy's pockets throughout and had passed unnoticed by the Royal Anglians' Medical Officer, Dr Swords, and others who had examined the body; secondly that the bombs had been deliberately planted on the body by some unknown person after the Medical Officer's examination. These possibilities were exhaustively examined in evidence because, although the matter is a relatively unimportant detail of the events of the afternoon, it is no doubt of great concern to Donaghy's family. I think that on a balance of probabilities the bombs were in Donaghy's pockets throughout. His jacket and trousers were not removed but were merely opened as he lay on his back in the car. It seems likely that these relatively bulky objects would have been noticed when Donaghy's body was examined;

but it is conceivable that they were not and the alternative explanation of a plant is mere speculation. No evidence was offered as to where the bombs might have come from, who might have placed them or why Donaghy should have been singled out for this treatment.

WERE THE SOLDIERS JUSTIFIED IN FIRING?

Troops on duty in Northern Ireland have standing instructions for opening fire. These instructions are set out upon the Yellow Card which every soldier is required to carry. Soldiers operating collectively—a term which is not itself defined—are not to open fire without an order from the Commander on the spot. Soldiers acting individually are generally required to give warning before opening fire and are subject to other general rules which provide *inter alia*:

2. Never use more force than the *minimum* necessary to enable you to carry out your duties.
3. Always first try to handle the situation by other means than opening fire. If you have to fire:
    (a) Fire only aimed shots.
    (b) Do not fire more rounds than are absolutely necessary to achieve your aim.

The injunction to fire only aimed shots is understood by the soldiers as ruling out shooting from the hip—which they in any case regard as inefficient, indeed pointless—except that in a very sudden emergency, requiring split-second action, a shot from the hip is regarded as permissible if it is as well aimed a shot as the circumstances allow.

Other stringent restrictions apply to soldiers who have given warning of intention to fire. But the rule of principal significance to the events of 30 January is that which contemplates a situation in which it is not practicable to give a warning. It provides:

You may fire without warning

13. Either when hostile firing is taking place in your area, and a warning is impracticable, or when any delay could lead to death or serious injury to people whom it is your duty to
    protect or to yourself; *and then only*:
    (a) against a person using a firearm against members of the security forces or people whom it is your duty to protect; or
    (b) against a person carrying a firearm if you have reason to think he is about to use it for offensive purposes.

The term "firearm" is defined as including a grenade, nail bomb or gelignite-type bomb.

Though no one has sought to criticise the spirit and intention of these orders, it would be optimistic to suppose that every soldier could be trained to understand them in detail and apply them rigidly. Even if he could, the terms of Rule 13 leave certain questions unanswered and, perhaps, unanswerable:

(i)   In the conditions contemplated by Rule 13, is fire to be opened defensively and restricted to that which is necessary to cause the attacker to desist and withdraw, or is he to be treated as an enemy in battle and engaged until he surrenders or is killed?

(ii)   In the like conditions, is fire to be withheld on account of risk to others in the vicinity who are not themselves carrying or using firearms? Suppose that in a crowd of youths throwing stones one is identified as holding a nail bomb. Is the soldier then to hold his fire because of risk to those who are only throwing stones?

(iii)   When hostile fire is taking place, how certain must the soldier be in identifying an object as a firearm? From the front a camera with a telescopic lens may look very much like certain types of sub-machine gun. A television sound recordist holding his microphone aloft could well be taken for someone about to throw a nail bomb. Faced with such a situation does the soldier wait or does he give himself the benefit of the doubt and fire?

Furthermore, anomalous situations could arise from the Yellow Card's definition of a firearm. Although the definition does not embrace the petrol bomb, the soldier is authorised to fire against a person throwing a petrol bomb, but only after due warning and if petrol bomb attacks continue and if the thrower's action is likely to endanger life. There is no specific mention of other types of missile, including acid bombs. However, the soldier is authorised to fire, after due warning, "*against a person attacking* . . . if his action is likely *to endanger life*", or "if there is no other way" for the soldier to protect himself or others "from the danger of being killed or seriously injured". So it would presumably be in order under the Yellow Card rules for a soldier to fire on a person hurling bricks or acid bombs or pieces of angle iron from high up on a tall building, but only after giving due warning, which it might not be easy to give.

Many people will be surprised to learn that it is not open to the soldier to give warning by firing warning shots. As has already been seen, the soldier is required to "fire only aimed shots". Whilst the Yellow Card does not in terms forbid a soldier hard-pressed by an advancing mob to fire over their heads, to do so is certainly a breach of the orders. The justification put forward for this somewhat surprising provision is that hooligans would rapidly note and take advantage of the regular firing of shots meant to pass harmlessly by; the carrying of firearms would cease to deter.

Soldiers will react to the situations in which they find themselves in different ways according to their temperament and to the prevailing circumstances. The more intensive the shooting or stone-throwing which is going on the more ready will they be to interpret the Yellow Card as permitting them to open fire. The individual soldier's reaction may also be affected by the general understanding of these problems which prevails in his unit. In the Parachute Regiment, at any rate in the 1st Battalion, the soldiers are trained to take what may be described as a hard line upon these questions. The events of 30 January and the attitude of individual soldiers whilst giving evidence suggest that when engaging an identified gunman or bomb-thrower they shoot to kill and continue to fire until the target disappears or falls. When under attack and returning fire they show no particular concern for the safety of others in the vicinity of the target. They are aware that civilians who do not wish to be associated with violence tend to make themselves scarce at the first alarm and they know that it is the deliberate policy of gunmen to use civilians as cover. Further, when hostile firing is taking place the soldiers of 1 Para will fire on a person who appears to be using a firearm against them without always waiting until they can positively identify the weapon. A more restrictive interpretation of the terms of the Yellow Card by 1 Para might have saved some of the casualties on 30 January, but with correspondingly increased risk to the soldiers themselves.

In the events which took place on 30 January the soldiers were entitled to regard themselves as acting individually and thus entitled to fire under the terms of Rule 13 without waiting for orders. Although it is true that Support Company operated as a Company with all its officers present, in the prevailing noise and confusion it was not practicable for officers or NCOs always to control the fire of individual soldiers. The soldiers' training certainly required them to act individually in such circumstances and no breach of discipline was thereby involved. I have already stated that in my view the initial firing by civilians in the courtyard of Rossville Flats was not heavy; but the immediate response of the soldiers produced a brisk and noisy engagement which must have had its effect on troops and civilians in Rossville Street. Civilian, as well as Army, evidence made it clear that there was a substantial number of civilians in the area who were armed with firearms. I would not be surprised if in the relevant half hour as many rounds were fired at the troops as were fired by them. The soldiers escaped injury by reason of their superior field-craft and training.

When the shooting began every soldier was looking for a gunman and he was his own judge of whether he had identified one or not. I have the explanation on oath of every soldier who fired for every round for which he was required to account. Were they truthfully recounting the facts as they saw them? If so, did those facts justify the action taken?

Those accustomed to listening to witnesses could not fail to be impressed by the demeanour of the soldiers of 1 Para. They gave their evidence with confidence and without hesitation or prevarication and withstood a rigorous cross-examination without contradicting themselves or each other. With one or two exceptions I accept that they were telling the truth as they remembered it. But did they take sufficient care before firing and was their conduct justified, even if the circumstances were as they described them?

There were infringements of the rules of the Yellow Card. Lieutenant N fired three rounds over the heads of a threatening crowd and dispersed it. Corporal P did likewise. Soldier T, on the authority of Sergeant O, fired at a person whom he believed to be throwing acid bombs and Soldier V said he fired on a petrol bomber. Although these actions were not authorised by the Yellow Card they do not seem to point to a breakdown in discipline or to require censure. Indeed, in three of the four cases it could be held that the person firing was, as the senior officer or NCO on the spot, the person entitled to give orders for such firing.

Grounds put forward for identifying gunmen at windows were sometimes flimsy. Thus Soldier F fired three rounds at a window in Rossville Flats after having been told by another soldier that there was a gunman there. He did not seem to have verified the information except by his observation of "a movement" at the window. Whether or not it was fired by Soldier H a round went through the window of a house in Glenfada Park into an empty room. The only people in the house were an old couple who happily were sitting in another room. In all 17 rounds were fired at the windows of flats and houses, not counting Soldier H's 19 rounds.

The identification of supposed nail bombers was equally nebulous—perhaps necessarily so. A nail bomb looks very much like half a brick and often the only means of distinguishing between a stone-thrower and a nail-bomber is that a light enough stone may be thrown with a flexed elbow whereas a nail bomb is usually thrown with a straight arm as in a bowling action.

Even assuming a legitimate target, the number of rounds fired was sometimes excessive. Soldier S's firing of 12 rounds into the alleyway between Blocks 1 and 2 of the Rossville Flats seems to me to have been unjustifiably dangerous for people round about.

Nevertheless in the majority of cases the soldier gave an explanation which, if true, justified his action. A typical phrase is "I saw a civilian aiming what I thought was a firearm and I fired an aimed shot at him". In the main I accept these accounts as a faithful reflection of the soldier's recollection of the incident; but there is no simple way of deciding whether his judgment was at fault or whether his decision was conscientiously made. Some of the soldiers showed a high degree of responsibility. Examples of this are the experienced Sergeant K, already referred to, and the 18-year-old Soldier R. At the other end of the scale are some of the soldiers who fired in Glenfada Park in the circumstances described above. Between these extremes a judgment must be based on the general impression of the soldiers' attitudes as a whole. There is no question of the soldiers firing in panic to protect their own skins. They were far too steady for that. But where soldiers are required to engage gunmen who are in close proximity to innocent civilians they are set an impossible task. Either they must go all out for the gunmen, in which case the innocent suffer; or they must put the safety of the innocent first, in which case many gunmen will escape and the risk to themselves will be increased. The only unit whose attitude to this problem I have examined is 1 Para. Other units may or may not be the same. In 1 Para the soldiers are trained to go for the gunmen and make their decisions quickly. In these circumstances it is not remarkable that mistakes were made and some innocent civilians hit.

In reaching these conclusions I have not been unmindful of the numerous allegations of misconduct by individual soldiers which were made in the course of the evidence. I considered that allegations of brutality by the soldiers in the course of making arrests were outside my terms of reference. There is no doubt that people who resisted or tried to avoid arrest were apt to be roughly handled; but whether excessive force was used is something which I have not investigated.

There have also been numerous allegations of soldiers firing carelessly from the hip or shooting deliberately at individuals who were clearly unarmed. These were all isolated allegations in which the soldier was not identified and which I could not investigate further. If, and insofar as, such incidents occurred the soldier in question must have accounted for the rounds fired by giving some different and lying story of how they were expended. Though such a possibility cannot be excluded, in general the accounts given by the soldiers of the circumstances in which they fired and the reasons why they did so were, in my opinion, truthful.

SUMMARY OF CONCLUSIONS

There would have been no deaths in Londonderry on 30 January if those who organised the illegal march had not thereby created a highly dangerous situation in which a clash between demonstrators and the security forces was almost inevitable.

The decision to contain the march within the Bogside and Creggan had been opposed by the Chief Superintendent of Police in Londonderry but was fully justified by events and was successfully carried out.

If the Army had persisted in its "low-key" attitude and had not launched a large-scale operation to arrest hooligans the day might have passed off without serious incident.

The intention of the senior Army officers to use 1 Para as an arrest force and not for other offensive purposes was sincere.

An arrest operation carried out in Battalion strength in circumstances in which the troops were likely to come under fire involved hazard to civilians in the area which Commander 8 Brigade may have underestimated.

The order to launch the arrest operation was given by Commander 8 Brigade. The tactical details were properly left to CO 1 Para who did not exceed his orders. In view of the experience of the unit in operations of this kind it was not necessary for CO 1 Para to give orders in greater detail than he did.

When the vehicles and soldiers of Support Company appeared in Rossville Street they came under fire. Arrests were made; but in a very short time the arrest operation took second place and the soldiers turned to engage their assailants. There is no reason to suppose that the soldiers would have opened fire if they had not been fired upon first.

Soldiers who identified armed gunmen fired upon them in accordance with the standing orders in the Yellow Card. Each soldier was his own judge of whether he had identified a gunman. Their training made them aggressive and quick in decision and some showed more restraint in opening fire than others. At one end of the scale some soldiers showed a high degree of responsibility; at the other, notably in Glenfada Park, firing bordered on the reckless. These distinctions reflect differences in the character and temperament of the soldiers concerned.

The standing orders contained in the Yellow Card are satisfactory. Any further restrictions on opening fire would inhibit the soldier from taking proper steps for his own safety and that of his comrades and unduly hamper the engagement of gunmen.

None of the deceased or wounded is proved to have been shot whilst handling a firearm or bomb. Some are wholly acquitted of complicity in such action; but there is a strong suspicion that some others had been firing weapons or handling bombs in the course of the afternoon and that yet others had been closely supporting them.

There was no general breakdown in discipline. For the most part the soldiers acted as they did because they thought their orders required it. No order and no training can ensure that a soldier will always act wisely, as well as bravely and with initiative. The individual soldier ought not to have to bear the burden of deciding whether to open fire in confusion such as prevailed on 30 January. In the conditions prevailing in Northern Ireland, however, this is often inescapable.

WIDGERY

W. J. Smith, *Secretary*
10 April, 1972

LIST OF WITNESSES

Civilians from Londonderry and area

Mrs M Bonnor	C McDaid
J G Bradley	P McDaid
M P Bridge	Mrs B McGuigan
J Carr	A Nash
J Chapman	P O'Donnell
J Doherty	W O'Reilly
Mrs I Duffy	J W Porter

F P Dunne

J Friel

J Gorman

W V Hegarty

J Johnson

F Lawton

Mrs M McCartney

G McCauley

M Quinn

Miss G F C Richmond

R M Rogan

Brother F B Sharpe

J Stevenson

D T Tucker

R A Wood

H L Young

Priests

Father D Bradley

Father E K Daly

Father J Irwin

Father M McIvor

Father V A Mulvey

Father T O'Gara

Father T M O'Keefe

Other civilians

L Bedell

Lord Brockway

Press and television reporters, photographers etc.

P E C Beggin

J D Bierman

D Capper

B Cashinella

C Cave

J A Chartres

C J Donnelly

C Doyle

F Grimaldi

R E Hammond

C Haslett

N Kunioka

W J Mailey

J P Morris

G Peress

D Phillips

G W H K Seymour

D S Tereshchuk

N H Wade

P F Wilkinson

S B A Winchester

Soldiers

Major General R C Ford, CBE
Brigadier A P W MacLellan, MBE
Lieutenant Colonel M C M Steele
Lieutenant Colonel P M Welsh
Lieutenant Colonel D Wilford

A	T
B	U
C	V
D	Y
E	AA
F	SAP
G	015
H	028
J	030
K	104
L	119
M	127
N	138
O	150
P	201
Q	227
R	236
S	

Police officers

Assistant Chief Constable R G Ca.npbell
Chief Superintendent F Lagan
Superintendent S McGonigle
Police Constable H B McCormac

Police Constable J Montgomery
PN7
PN93
PS34

Doctors, forensic experts and pathologists

Dr D J L Carson	Dr J R Press
Dr T K Marshall	Prof K Simpson
Dr J Martin	Dr P J K Swords

LEGAL REPRESENTATIVES

Counsel for the Tribunal
Mr J Stocker QC
Mr L Read
Mr T W Preston
    (instructed by the Treasury Solicitor)

Counsel for the Ministry of Defence
Mr E B Gibbens QC
Mr M Underhill
  (instructed by the Army Legal Services)

Counsel for the next of kin of twelve of the deceased and for the injured
Mr J McSparran QC
Mr R C Hill
  (instructed by Mr C Napier on behalf of the next of kin and by Mr B McCluskey on behalf of the injured)

Counsel for the Londonderry priests
Mr W McCollum QC
Mr P Mooney
  (instructed by Messrs Maxwell & Co.)

Counsel for Mr S B A Winchester
Mr G P M Gibson
  (instructed by Messrs Johns, Elliot and Wallace)

For Independent Television News
Mr C F B Winder of Messrs Biddle and Co.

Other titles in the series

The Amritsar Massacre: General Dyer in the Punjab, 1919

"We feel that General Dyer, by adopting an inhuman and un-British method of dealing with subjects of His Majesty the King-Emperor, has done great disservice to the interest of British rule in India. This aspect it was not possible for the people of the mentality of General Dyer to realise."

Backdrop

At the time of the events described, India was under British rule. Indians had fought alongside the British in the First World War, and had made tremendous financial contributions to the British war effort. Mahatma Gandhi was the leader of the Indian National Congress party, which was seeking independence from the British Empire.

The Book

This is the story of the action taken by Brigadier-General Dyer at Amritsar in the Punjab in 1919. Faced with insurrection in support of Mahatma Gandhi, the British Army attempted to restore order. General Dyer, on arriving in the troubled city of Amritsar, issued an order banning any assembly of more than four people. Consequently, when he discovered a large crowd gathered together during a cattle fair, he took the astonishing action of shooting more than three hundred unarmed people. Regarding the subsequent native obedience as a satisfactory result, he was surprised to find himself removed from command a year later, and made lengthy representations to Parliament.

ISBN 0 11 702412 0   Price £6.99

British Battles of World War I, 1914–15

"The effect of these poisonous gases was so virulent as to render the whole of the line held by the French Division incapable of any action at all. It was at first impossible for anyone to realise what had actually happened. The smoke and fumes hid everything from sight, and hundreds of men were thrown into a comatose or dying condition, and within an hour the whole position had to be abandoned, together with about 50 guns."

Backdrop
On 4 August 1914, Britain declared war on Germany. Germany had already invaded Belgium and France and was progressing towards Paris.

The Book
These are the despatches from some of the battles of the first two years of World War I. They include action in northern France, Germany, Gallipoli, and even as far afield as the Cocos Islands in the Indian Ocean. They describe the events of battle, the tremendous courage, the huge losses, and the confusions and difficulties of war. These startling accounts, which were written by the generals at the front, were first published in the "London Gazette", the official newspaper of Parliament.

ISBN 0 11 702447 3   Price £6.99

Florence Nightingale and the Crimea, 1854–55

"By an oversight, no candles were included among the stores brought to the Crimea. Lamps and wicks were brought but not oil. These omissions were not supplied until after possession had been taken of Balaklava, and the purveyor had an opportunity of purchasing candles and oil from the shipping and the dealers in the town."

Backdrop
The British Army arrived in the Crimea in 1854, ill-equipped to fight a war in the depths of a Russian winter.

The Book
The hospital service for wounded soldiers during the Crimean War was very poor and became the subject of concern, not just in the army, but also in the press. "The Times" was publishing letters from the families of soldiers describing the appalling conditions. This embarrassed the government, but even more it irritated the army, which did not know how to cope with such open scrutiny of its activities.

The book is a collection of extracts from government papers published in 1855 and 1856. Their selection provides a snapshot of events at that time. In particular they focus on the terrible disaster that was the Charge of the Light Brigade, and the inadequate provisions that were made for the care of the sick and wounded. The documents relating to the hospitals at Scutari include evidence from Florence Nightingale herself.

ISBN 0 11 702425 2   Price £6.99

Lord Kitchener and Winston Churchill: The Dardanelles Commission Part I, 1914–15

"The naval attack on the Narrows was never resumed. It is difficult to understand why the War Council did not meet between 19th March and 14th May. The failure of the naval attack showed the necessity of abandoning the plan of forcing the passage of the Dardanelles by purely naval operation. The War Council should then have met and considered the future policy to be pursued."

Backdrop

The Dardanelles formed part of the main southern shipping route to Russia, and was of great military and strategic importance. However, it had long been recognised by the British naval and military authorities that any attack on the Dardanelles would be an operation fraught with great difficulties.

The Book

During the early stages of World War I, Russia made a plea to her allies to make a demonstration against the Turks. So attractive was the prize of the Dardanelles to the British generals, notably Lord Kitchener, that this ill-fated campaign was launched. Just how powerful an influence Kitchener was to exert over the War Council, and just how ill-prepared the Allies were to conduct such an attack, are revealed in dramatic detail in the report of this Commission.

The book covers the first part of the Commission's report. It deals with the origin, inception and conduct of operations in the Dardanelles from the beginning of the war in August 1914 until March 1915, when the idea of a purely naval attack was abandoned.

ISBN 0 11 702423 6   Price £6.99

The Russian Revolution, 1917

"It is the general opinion in Ekaterinburg that the Empress, her son, and four daughters were not murdered, but were despatched on the 17th July to the north or the west. The story that they were burnt in a house seems to be an exaggeration of the fact that in a wood outside the town was found a heap of ashes, apparently the result of burning a consider-able amount of clothing. At the bottom of the ashes was a diamond, and, as one of the Grand Duchesses is said to have sewn a diamond into the lining of her cloak, it is supposed that the clothes of the Imperial family were burnt there."

Backdrop

By November 1917 Russia had lost more than twenty million people in the war. Lenin's Bolshevik party had overthrown the Tsar and had called for an end to all capitalist governments.

The Book

Government files contain a number of detailed documents describing the nature of the Bolshevik Revolution and the gov-ernment of Lenin, which was observed to be not only abhorrent but also menacing because of the international implications. The book is compiled from two of these files, one of which describes the events leading up to the revolution and how the Bolsheviks came to power in October 1917. The other contains a series of eye-witness accounts of the frightening days of the Bolshevik regime from the summer of 1918 to April 1919.

ISBN 0 11 702424 4   Price £6.99

UFOs in the House of Lords, 1979

"Is it not time that Her Majesty's Government informed our people of what they know about UFOs? The UFOs have been coming in increasing numbers for 30 years since the war, and I think it is time our people were told the truth. We have not been invaded from outer space. Most incidents have not been hostile. Indeed it is us, the earthlings, who have fired on them. … Whatever the truth is, I am sure that an informed public is a prepared one. Another thing: it is on record that both sighting and landing reports are increasing all the time. Just suppose the 'ufonauts' decided to make mass landings tomorrow in this country – there could well be panic here, because our people have not been prepared."

Backdrop
The winter of 1978/79 in Britain was a time of strikes and unrest. It became known as the "winter of discontent". Yet it seems that the House of Lords had other more important things to discuss.

The Book
The book is the transcript of a debate in the House of Lords which took place in February 1979. Their Lordships debated the need for an international initiative in response to the problem of Unidentified Flying Objects. There were several notable speeches from noble lords and distinguished prelates.

ISBN 0 11 702413 9   Price £6.99

D Day to VE Day: General Eisenhower's Report, 1944–45

"During the spring of 1945, as the sky grew darker over Germany, the Nazi leaders had struggled desperately, by every means in their power, to whip their people into a last supreme effort to stave off defeat, hoping against hope that it would be possible, if only they could hold out long enough, to save the day by dividing the Allies. Blinded as they were by their own terror and hatred of 'Bolshevism', they were incapable of understanding the strength of the bond of common interest existing between Britain, the United States and the Soviet Union."

Backdrop

In 1944 the Allies were poised to launch an attack against Hitler's German war machine. The planning and timing were crucial. In February, General Eisenhower was appointed Supreme Commander of the Allied Operations in Europe.

The Book

The book is Dwight D. Eisenhower's personal account of the Allied invasion of Europe, from the preparations for the D-Day landings in Normandy, France, to the final assault across Germany. He presents a story of a far more arduous struggle than is commonly portrayed against an enemy whose tenacity he admired and whose skills he feared. It is a tactical account of his understanding of enemy manoeuvres, and his attempts to counter their actions. The formality of the report is coloured by many personal touches, and the reader senses Eisenhower's growing determination to complete the task. Hindsight would have had the general take more notice of Russian activity, but that this was not obvious to him is one of the fascinations of such a contemporary document.

ISBN 0 11 702451 1 Price £6.99

The Irish Uprising, 1914–21: Papers from the British Parliamentary Archive

"Captain Bowen-Colthurst adopted the extraordinary, and indeed almost meaningless, course of taking Mr Sheehy Skeffington with him as a 'hostage'. He had no right to take Mr Sheehy Skeffington out of the custody of the guard for this or any other purpose, and he asked no one's leave to do so. Before they left the barracks Mr Sheehy Skeffington's hands were tied behind his back and Captain Bowen-Colthurst called upon him to say his prayers. Upon Mr Sheehy Skeffington refusing to do so Captain Bowen-Colthurst ordered the men of his party to take their hats off and himself uttered a prayer, the words of it being: 'O Lord God, if it shall please thee to take away the life of this man, forgive him for Christ's sake.'"

Backdrop

In 1914 it was still the case that the whole of Ireland was part of Great Britain, under the dominion of the King, and Irish constituencies were represented in the British Parliament.

The Book

This book contains five remarkable documents published by the British Government between 1914 and 1921, relating to the events leading up to the partition of Ireland in 1921. In the first, a report is made into the shooting of civilians following a landing of arms at Howth outside Dublin. The second is of the papers discovered relating to the activities of Sinn Fein and particularly of Sir Roger Casement. The third is the government inquiry into the Easter Rising of 1916. The fourth describes the treatment of three journalists by the British Army shortly after the uprising, and the last is an exchange of correspondence between Eamon de Valera and David Lloyd George prior to the Anglo-Irish Treaty of 1921.

ISBN 0 11 702415 5   Price £6.99

The Siege of the Peking Embassy, 1900

"I cannot conclude this despatch without saying a word of praise respecting the ladies of all nationalities who so ably and devotedly assisted the defence, notwithstanding the terrible shadow which at all times hung over the legation – a shadow which the never-ceasing rattle of musketry and crash of round shot and shell and the diminishing number of defenders rendered ever present. They behaved with infinite patience and cheerfulness, helping personally in the hospital or, in making sandbags and bandages, and in assisting in every possible way the work of defence. Especially commended are two young ladies – Miss Myers and Miss Daisy Brazier – who daily filtered the water for the hospital, in tropical heat, and carried it with bullets whistling and shells bursting in the trees overhead." Sir Claude MacDonald

The Backdrop
The Boxer movement in China was a secret society which preached hatred of foreigners. By the spring of 1900, this movement was out of control. On 9 June, the Boxers launched their first attack against foreign property in Peking by burning down the racecourse. On 19 June, all foreigners were order to evacuate Peking within 24 hours. The order was not complied with.

The Book
As events worsened for the diplomats and their families in Peking, Sir Claude MacDonald, the British ambassador, wired the Admiralty in Taku to request the immediate despatch of a relief force. Just how that relief force fared, and how the hundreds of diplomats and their families who were stranded inside the Legation buildings coped with the rigours of the siege, are the subject of the diplomatic papers presented in this book. The central part of the story is the gripping diary of events kept by Sir Claude MacDonald.

ISBN 0 11 702456 2   Price £6.99

The Siege of Kars, 1855

"We had, up to that date, suffered from cold, want of sufficient clothing, and starvation, without a murmur escaping from the troops. They fell dead at their posts, in their tents, and throughout the camp as brave men should who cling to their duty through the slightest glimmering of hope of saving a place entrusted to their custody. From the day of their glorious victory on 29th September, they had not tasted animal food, and their nourishment consisted of two-fifths of a ration of bread and the roots of grass, which they scarcely had the strength to dig for; yet night and day they stood to their arms, their wasted frames showing the fearful effects of starvation, but their sparkling eye telling me what they would do were the enemy to attack them again." W. F. Williams

Backdrop
In 1855, while the British Army was fighting alongside the French and the Turkish armies in the Crimean War, a little-known but serious siege was taking place in the city of Kars in eastern Turkey. Set within mountains and overlooking a gorge, Kars is a natural fortress, but its possession by the Turks was threatened by the Russians.

The Book
During the Crimean War, the British were giving aid to the Turkish army by lending them generals to help organise and strengthen their garrisons. General Williams had arrived in Kars in September 1854, having been appointed British Military Commissioner with the Turkish Army in Asia. He soon began organising the troops there, although his repeated requests for supplies and reinforcements were met with delay and obfuscation. These despatches concerning the siege of Kars date from May 1855. Their unfolding tells a sorry tale of heroism and frustrated hope.

ISBN 0 11 702454 6   Price £6.99

Defeat at Gallipoli: The Dardanelles Commission Part II, 1915–16

"It has been represented . . . that from a military point of view, the Dardanelles Expedition, even if unsuccessful, was justified by the fact that it neutralised or contained a large number of Turkish troops who otherwise would have been free to operate elsewhere. Lord Kitchener estimated this number as being nearly 300,000. But in containing the Turkish force, we employed . . . a total of at least 400,000. Our casualties amounted to 31,389 killed, 78,749 wounded and 9,708 missing, making a total of 119,846. The expedition also involved heavy financial expenditure and the employment of a considerable naval force."

Backdrop
The naval attempt by the British to force the Dardanelles was abandoned in March 1915. Rather than losing face, the military commanders decided to send a large army to the area.

The Book
Picking up the story from where the earlier volume, *Lord Kitchener and Winston Churchill*, left off, this second part of the Dardanelles Commission's report deals with the disastrous military campaign to capture the Gallipoli Peninsula using ground forces. As the story unfolds, we learn how the Allies were unable to make any headway against an enemy who was well prepared and well positioned. Within a few months the Allies had suffered a humiliating defeat, and thousands of men had lost their lives. The realisation of the government's incompetence in handling this affair was instrumental in the removal of Herbert Asquith as Prime Minister in December 1916.

ISBN 0 11 702455 4   Price £6.99

Travels in Mongolia, 1902: A Journey by C.W. Campbell, the British Consul in China

"I took that road on 3rd June 1902. It is necessary to be precise about dates, because the aspect of this plain varies enormously with the season. It was now in summer dress, a restful assortment of greens; but the heat was not yet of the monsoon, for which the farmers were longing. The country was parched. No rain had fallen for a fortnight and the millet was bleaching. The roads, channels of dull ochre, were insufferable from dust; the pools had shrunk to patches of crust, and there was nothing to lay the impalpable powder, a blend of loss and alluvium, which the heated breeze kept in suspension."

Backdrop

In the years following the Boxer Rebellion of 1900, there were several consular missions to remote parts of China. Here there were large tracts of land, still largely unexplored by Western travellers.

The Book

The purpose of Mr Campbell's journey through Mongolia isn't immediately obvious, but the description he imparts is still as fresh and vivid today as when he first wrote it. On this particular journey, Consul Campbell travels north from Peking around the fringe of the Gobi Desert and into Mongolia. *En route* he records the history, landscape and way of life of those he meets. There is no doubt that his gift for describing the beauty he perceived would have been a source of delight to his readers at home.

ISBN 0 11 702452 X   Price £6.99

John Profumo and Christine Keeler

"The story must start with Stephen Ward, aged fifty. The son of a clergymen, by profession he was an osteopath ... his skill was very considerable and he included among his patients many well-known people ... Yet at the same time he was utterly immoral."

The Backdrop
The beginning of the '60s saw the publication of *Lady Chatterley's Lover* and the dawn of sexual and social liberation as traditional morals began to be questioned and in some instances swept away.

The Book
In spite of the recent spate of political falls from grace, the Profumo Affair remains the biggest scandal ever to hit British politics. The Minister of War was found to be having an affair with a call girl who had associations with a Russian naval officer at the height of the Cold War. There are questions of cover-up, lies told to Parliament, bribery and stories sold to the newspapers. Lord Denning's superbly written report into the scandal describes with astonishment and fascinated revulsion the extraordinary sexual behaviour of the ruling classes. Orgies, naked bathing, sado–masochistic gatherings of the great and good and ministers and judges cavorting in masks are all uncovered.

ISBN 0 11 702402 3   Price £6.99